Love, Duty and Escape: Italy 1943

Inspired by the untold true account of Captain R.E. Selby's survival in WWII

C. D. Hallpike-Selby

Helion & Company

Helion & Company Limited
Unit 8 Amherst Business Centre
Budbrooke Road
Warwick
CV34 5WE
England
Tel. 01926 499619
Email: info@helion.co.uk
Website: www.helion.co.uk
X (formerly Twitter): @Helionbooks
Facebook: @HelionBooks
Visit our blog at helionbooks.wordpress.com

Published by Helion & Company 2025
Designed and typeset by Mach 3 Solutions (www.mach3solutions.co.uk)
Cover designed by Paul Hewitt, Battlefield Design (www.battlefield-design.co.uk)

ISBN 978-1-804518-79-3

British Library Cataloguing-in-Publication Data.
A catalogue record for this book is available from the British Library.

For details of other military history titles published by Helion & Company Limited, contact the
above address, or visit our website: http://www.helion.co.uk

We always welcome receiving book proposals from prospective authors.

This story is dedicated to every 'local lad and lass' on whose courage and sacrifice the liberty of following generations has been built.

Love, Duty and Escape: Italy 1943

Reginald Edward Selby, 1920-2005, aged 23. (Family Archive)

This book tells the true story of the World War II capture and escape of Captain Reginald Edward Selby based on the personal testimony and on previously unknown documents – a tale of love, danger and honour. It recounts the bravery of soldiers, partisans and citizens, set in the beautiful Italian landscape around Pellegrino Parmense, near Parma, hilltop home of cheese, wine and honey…

Contents

Illustrations

Photographs – The military photographs are from the suitcase of documents left to the family by Reg. The location photographs from 1987 are reproduced by kind permission of Claire Diana Hallpike-Selby. The photograph of the Round House Lodge is courtesy of Reginal Selby, taken in 1988.

Maps – Maps are added to provide guidance to the reader:
Mediterranean Sea showing North Africa and Italy
Overview of Italy showing the location of Parma relative to Rome and Milan and the border with Switzerland
Local map showing Parma and the villages key to this story: Fontanellato, Pellegrino Parmense and Varano Marchesi.

Documents – Other documents are drawn directly from the suitcase of materials left by Reg.

Acknowledgements

Our thanks to those kind Italians in Emilia-Romagna who sat with us, talked with us and drank wine with us on the research journeys in 1987. We particularly want to thank the assistant barber, Paolo, in Fontanellato who as a teenager in 1942 had sharpened the tools for the main barber to the camp during the war and who, four decades later, recounted how he had broken the curfew and raced out at night to collect Red Cross parcels in the fields. Likewise, our thanks go to Giorgio Frati who led us to him, and shared with us his own memories as a seven-year-old in 1942 – together with some of the delicious local *rosso* mentioned here too.

The 1987 research trip was undertaken on a tandem. This meant that we felt the rise and fall of the landscape in a very direct physical way, bringing us closer to the tough lives and experiences of the *partigiani*, and of Reg Selby and his fellow escaped POWs. It also ensured a closer, warmer reception from the villagers – once it was clear that we were from England!

Our thanks must go to Claudio in Salsomaggiore, who repaired our transport, the tandem, for the equivalent in Lire of just £2.50, his wild hair and green eyes enchanting us. In fact, further thanks are due to Claudio for also rescuing our money pouch, forgotten and left behind in a blue plastic bag at the castle on our last stop before the tandem broke down, along with our shopping of cheese and water from the local *latteria*.

I am also grateful to Malcolm Tudor for the tireless research he has done into collating the reports from escaping POWs in his collection of works on the subject. Contemporary details from his research into many parallel escape reports are incorporated here where appropriate to add touches of everyday life that colour and support Reg's core story, as told by him in his own personal notes.

Lieutenant R. Selby of the Bedfordshire and Hertfordshire Regiment is in fact mentioned as one of the successful escapees helped at some point by the family of Malcolm Tudor's mother, Clara Dall'Arda, on page 123 of the book *British Prisoners of War in Italy: Paths to Freedom*. Their family name is not included in Reg's list of helpers and days hosted. Perhaps this confirms that there were yet more families besides those named in this account, whose generosity and bravery were not individually recorded in his notes but which were nonetheless much appreciated and represent the 'others' category on his list.

The names of those helpers Reg had noted down were contained in his official report, delivered to the British Authorities at Wil in Switzerland after his successful escape. That list includes the name Ernesto Varani, who is also mentioned by Malcolm Tudor as having assisted the escapees. Amongst the names of other escapees that overlap in these accounts is John Baddeley.

Norton Brabourne is also specifically recalled in Reg Selby's notes as billeted to the same hut in the prisoner-of-war camp south of Naples. Major Young who was captured with Reg in Africa and travelled with him to Naples, was not included in the transfer to Fontanellato. Reg did not hear what happened to him after that. It is possible that the Communist Partisan leader was either Emilio Robuschi or Remo Polizzi, who were in the local resistance teams described by Malcolm Tudor in the same book.

It was rewarding to read the reference to 'The Accountant' in the wartime memoire, *Love and War in the Apennines* by Eric Newby, another inmate of Camp PG49, as helpful evidence of a link to a fellow POW.

My editorial thanks go to the publisher and also to professional editor, Julie Dyson for her perceptive comments, her thorough and accurate error correction and her untiring support in helping me battle with combining the different voices in the book. I also extend my sincere gratitude to Erica Saracino for checking the Italian words and phases included in the text.

Disclaimer

While many of the events and characters in this book are based on direct reports, the narrative is elaborated and fictionalised for the purposes of the story. No offence is intended and any inadvertent errors in those original statements may be due to fading memory or misinterpretation, for which the author is not responsible.

Preface and Introduction

When nineteen-year-old Reg Selby signed up to serve his country shortly after the outbreak of war in 1939, the weight of expectation lay heavy on his young shoulders. His father, Edward Selby, had won the Distinguished Service Medal for conspicuous gallantry in World War One. Would Reg ever be able to meet his father's expectations? Would he, indeed, even survive?

Reginald's untold story is one of courage in battle, capture in Africa, escape from a prisoner-of-war camp in Italy in September 1943, life and love in rural Italy, then finally the long, hard and terrifying journey to liberty with the help of the partisans, the *partigiani*.

In common with so many survivors of the brutal 1939–1945 global conflict, Reg spoke very little about his war. Captain R. E. Selby did not however let go of the documents that traced his experiences. He kept the papers, both official and unofficial, public and private, handwritten notes, jottings and photographs that bore witness to the memories that were so significant for him from that time. When the war was over and he was back in civilian life, Reg, like so many soldiers, simply wanted to live, and enjoy, the life which luck had allowed him to keep. Reginald Selby, personal number 197146, Army number 5955945, put his war away, locking the papers in an old leather suitcase and confining his memories to the back of his mind.

Reg's personal account of his wartime experiences was written down in 1986 from notes and documents he had kept in that old, brown leather suitcase. This book is a retelling of the story that draws not only on those original notes but also on subsequent research by younger members of his family, both during investigative trips undertaken with those notes in 1987 and later in the early 2000s, as well as from a range of other historical military sources.

In anticipation of their 1987 visit to Italy, Reg explained that his greatest wish was to find out if those brave and selfless Italians who had helped him had themselves escaped retribution. He wanted his family to understand the gratitude he felt to the ordinary folk who had risked their lives to help him survive. He also wanted us to know about a romantic relationship that had blossomed there and which he still recalled with tender affection.

Yet still he withheld the suitcase of documents and images that bore witness to the intense experiences of the years of his wartime service. It was only in his last months of life that the documents, letters and maps were discovered in a small, leather suitcase that he had kept unopened in the loft of the family home for many decades. His granddaughter, Zenia, first reviewed those documents after he had passed away, and her work has contributed to making this expanded account of his story accessible to a new generation.

In this book, the material is structured as an unfolding story, so that new generations of his family as well as other young readers can engage with it as an experience rather than a series of facts. Certain literary devices have been used to keep the storyline clear for the modern reader. These also provide a framework that can incorporate all the research done by different people in different decades.

The narrative is led by a fictional granddaughter, whom I have called Beth. In the story, her experiences represent the actual journeys of discovery that in real life were undertaken in the 1980s by members of Reg's family.

In this fictionalised narrative, Beth pieces together the threads of her grandfather's wartime story using – just as Reg's actual family had done – the materials from the suitcase of documents that he left. In a timeframe set the year after his funeral, Beth makes her own journey to Italy to follow the trail of her grandfather for herself. In this journey the fictional Beth uncovers more information as she traces Reg's story by following the route used by real family members in 1987 and again with Reg's grandchildren later, and which mirrored much of Reg's own personal account. To help her in her endeavours, a further fictional character called Robert has been introduced.

Where minor changes have been made to the original account from Reg himself, the reasons for these are usually to assist in the flow of the narrative and without changing any confirmed facts.

A fitting introduction to this presentation of an untold true life story is perhaps the statement from Prime Minister, Winston Churchill himself:

> Out of about eighty thousand of these men, conspicuously clothed in battle dress, and in the main with little knowledge of the language or geography of the country, at least ten thousand, mostly helped by the local population with civilian clothes, were guided to safety, thanks to the risks taken by members of the Italian Resistance and the simple people of the countryside.

The bravery of the ordinary citizens of Italy during these years in helping Allied POWs was highlighted by Winston Churchill in his work, *The Second World War, Volume V: Closing the Ring*

A Very Brief Summary by The Author of The History of The Two World Wars for any Readers Unfamiliar with The Period

Some younger readers of this story may not be familiar with the history of the two world wars in the twentieth century. However, the impact and message of these conflicts continues to influence countries around the world today. The key elements of those terrible years for the purposes of this account, could be summarised as follows.

World War I

World War I, 1914–1919, caused the largest mass killing of humans, almost all of them men, through one conflict up to that point in history. This was partly because the traditional battle strategy of two armies meeting in a fixed place to fight each other until one side was declared victorious, collided with the invention of new weapons that could cause killing and maiming on a vast and horrendous scale never before seen. These weapons were machine guns, chemical bombs, ever-larger rocket-like cannon and later, the first aeroplanes and tanks. These weapons were used against a ground force consisting largely of human bodies and horses. This war, mainly fought within Europe, and begun by Austria and Serbia, quickly escalated into a conflict involving, Russia, Germany, France and the United Kingdom, and ultimately many more nations in locations across many continents.

Over the course of the war in Europe, millions of men on each side manned the battle lines by living in mud trenches in miserable conditions. To attack the enemy, they had to try to cross the neutral ground between the opposing trenches, which became known as no-man's-land. In due course, each side used the advanced weapons systems, leading to mass deaths for both forces. The horror that resulted was so extensive and so shocking that this was supposed to be 'the war to end all wars' and ensure that mankind would never want to experience the same again. The war was halted by an armistice at the eleventh hour on the eleventh day of the eleventh month in 1918, in part to symbolise how close humanity had come to irreversible disaster. (NB although the Armistice, essentially a truce and cease-fire, ran from 11 November 1918 it was initially for only 36 days and had to be extended three times before a Peace was finally signed on 28 June 1919 to formally end the war – hence we give the date of the war as 1914–1919).

World War II

Sadly, the message of peace was not heeded and World War II, of 1939 to 1945, followed less than a human generation later. This time, the conflict spread to involve nations all over the globe. Treaties of mutual military support had been put in place after the First World War to protect smaller nations and in theory deter would-be aggressors from initiating a new war. However, this had the consequence of obliging more nations to enter the fray, as soon as countries which were signatories to those pacts, were invaded.

The weaponry had advanced even further and the proliferation of the use of planes meant that civilians in territory outside the battlefields could now also be attacked. Cities were bombed, especially fire-bombed, to subdue the enemy population's support for the war – on both sides. Motorised transport was by now common, meaning that almost every region and town could be reached and affected by the fighting. The distance they could cover from the respective transport bases was limited only by the amount of fuel the armed machines could carry.

The war started in Europe with the aggressors being led from Germany by the Austrian politician, Adolf Hitler. His special guard of vicious and cruel henchmen became known as the Nazis, due to their extreme nationalist agenda. This included the goal of exterminating categories of people that they felt should not exist, most notably the Jews. Their industrial scale systematic capture and murder of these people in camps is referred to as the Holocaust and led to the global recognition of genocide as a crime against humanity. The opposing Allies were led by the United Kingdom. Initially, the Italians were allied to Germany but changed sides in September 1943, as this story describes.

By 1945, German resources were overstretched due to their having to fight the enemy allied forces on too many fronts. Meanwhile, the opposing Allied Armies, which were already flagging by the end of 1941, were boosted with money and men from the United States of America when it entered the war after the Japanese attack on the US Navy base at Pearl Harbour in Hawaii – United States' sovereign territory. The US, this super-power nation, provided vital support in the European arena, as well as fighting in the Asia Pacific region. After several more years of conflict, the Second World War ended in two stages: victory in Europe, with the defeat of an exhausted Germany and its allies; and a few months later, victory in Japan and the Asia Pacific. The latter success was achieved by the invention and use of the most terrifying new weapon of mass destruction that had ever been invented: the atomic bomb. Control of the development and use of that new device has been essential to the safety of the world since 1945, and remains crucial to the survival of humanity.

Like all major world events, these wars were made up both of big movements on a national and international scale and also of the myriad smaller actions and experiences of many, many individuals. This is one such record.

1

The Suitcase

Guarda qua, chistu ciardino
Siente, sì sti sciure arance
Nu profumo accussì fino
Dinto 'o core se ne va
E tu dici: "Io parto, addio!"
T'alluntane da stu core
Da sta terra de l'ammore
Tiene 'o core 'e nun turnà
Ma nun me lassà
Non darme sto tormiento
Torna a Surriento
Famme campà

See these beautiful gardens,
Breathe in the uniquely fine
Orange perfume that moves the heart –
And yet, you say, 'Farewell, I have to go,
I have to leave your side and this land of love
Where my heart belongs – never to return.'
But no, please, don't leave, don't give me such torment,
Come back to Sorrento, so I can live (again)!

Extract from the song *Come Back to Sorrento* by Ernesto de Curtis
(translation by Claire Diana Hallpike-Selby)

How could young Reg, an eighteen-year-old lad from Hertfordshire, have known what he would face, how his life would change as tanks rolled into Poland in September 1939? How could he guess that his love of vaulting over the garden gate instead of opening the latch would soon save his life – and yet set him on a new and dangerous journey?

A lifetime later, Beth, his granddaughter had no idea, as she prepared to join her family at his funeral that her settled world, her understanding of her dear grandfather, was about to be turned upside down. Unbeknown to her, today she would receive a small, brown suitcase that would set her on a journey of rediscovery.

Glancing at the time, she quickly picked up her small black handbag and pulled the door of her flat shut behind her. She had a long drive from London to the outskirts of Manchester ahead and this was not a day to arrive late.

A few hours later, she reversed her pink and grey Mini-Clubman carefully into the last small space on the lane outside the church. She stepped out of the car, her auburn curls bouncing on the shoulders of her tailored black jacket, and looked around to get her bearings and compose herself.

In the heart of the tiny, ancient village of Dunham Massey, Cheshire, drifts of sun-gold leaves blew gently across the lane by the old stone church. As she watched, the hearse, highly polished, sombre and black, rolled up to the lychgate of St Margaret's. In the warm sunshine of this early autumn day, it brought her grandad, Reginald Edward Selby on his last journey.

The assembling guests, family young and old, friends and former colleagues, had parked their cars all along the surrounding narrow country lanes. They walked from each direction, quietly converging on the small church, as if drawing in the decades of his life.

Inside, his three sons, all in their mid-to-late forties and wearing dark suits over crisply ironed white shirts, exchanged man-hugs. Their blue eyes were red-rimmed, and the strains of mourning were tracked in their faces. The eldest ran a nervous hand over a balding pate, already smooth like his father's. Greying temples in the mousy brown showed the marks of time on the second son, and the third flicked a blond streak back from a receding hairline to meet the grey that rose from the back of his starched collar.

Their wives, dressed in black, handed out Orders of Service and guided the deceased's elderly sister and sister-in-law, both called Kathleen, to pews near the front. The younger grandchildren stayed near their parents, while the teenagers stood awkwardly by the heavy old oak doors, not sure whether to smile or nod at their grandfather's stooped ex-colleagues and golfing buddies who shuffled carefully past and into the church.

Outside, Beth walked calmly and steadily past the hearse. Just a flicker of her damp lashes betrayed the emotion within. In a moment, she passed out of the sunlight and into the softly muted daylight and shadows of the church.

She paused just inside the entrance. Her grandmother, the widow, was standing there, hovering in the cool grey of the old stone church porch. Her bright blue eyes were fixed with tearful focus on the black figures opening and closing the doors of the hearse.

'Nanna,' said Beth, gently taking her grandmother by the arm and turning her away from the sight of the six pall bearers sliding the coffin carefully from the hearse. Her grandmother turned her head to look in the direction of her granddaughter, but without seeing. She gave an almost imperceptible nod in acceptance that it was time to take their seats. Then they walked slowly together, arm in arm, to the front pew. Two smartly-dressed women, who after lifetimes of sharing happy moments, now shared the grief of loss.

The soft sound of the organ was bringing a restful, melodic piece to a close. Beth picked up the Order of Service and studied the image on the cover. Then she noticed the wording on the cover with surprise, 'Nanna, it says *Captain* Reginald Edward Selby. I didn't know Grandad was in the army!'

'In the war, my dear – and when he was finally discharged, he was allowed to keep and use the title "Captain" if he chose to. He never used it in business life, but he was proud of it, so I thought it was right to remember it today.'

Beth frowned a little and stared at the photograph of her familiar grandfather below the well-known name and the unfamiliar title on the front of the folded booklet. She felt confused that she did not know about this distinction, so important to him that it stood before his name, his very identity, today.

The organ paused, then struck a new tone. Low notes sounded through the old building, vibrating as if rising from beneath the stone floor to shake the mourners from their reveries. The vicar called for everyone to stand, and the pall bearers made their steady way up the centre aisle of the traditional village church. The wooden casket with brass handles processed at a solemn pace by each carved wooden pew, marking a last pass down the aisle for the former church warden of many years. The bearers placed the coffin on the waiting stands at the front of the church and stepped respectfully away.

An emotional tribute from Reginald's eldest son and a warm eulogy from a long-standing friend were followed by hymns, prayers and a sermon from the vicar. Finally, the organ played *The Day Thou Gavest, Lord, is Ended* and the congregation tried to sing.

As the music played, Beth looked across at the faces in the pews. The episodes and themes of her grandfather's story seemed to strike a different chord with each person, triggering happy memories with some, or thoughts of struggles shared with others. The man who was 'Reg' to his friends, and 'Reggie' to his wife, was to Beth simply her beloved grandad – 'Dadu.' She looked down at the Order of Service again and could not help wondering if he had been known by another name in the army, maybe a nickname. Was he Captain Reg? Maybe some other name? Where had the war taken him? She glanced up at the rafters in their shadowy stripes, as if half-expecting them to whisper a response.

At work, Reginald Selby had been a respected company director in the emerging industry of computer hardware. He was, to many a client, a genial golfing buddy. At home, he was a loving hard-working husband, a long-suffering father of three sons, a diligent brother who bought a house for his unmarried sister Kathleen, a doting grandfather. And in his community he was a stalwart member of the Church.

As the service progressed, Beth heard highlights of days playing golf, of dinner-dances in the 1950s and 1960s, of his work on the 'new innovation' of desktop computers, and of how he never talked of his wartime experiences in Italy, though they were known to have influenced many of his decisions in life. She learnt that his love of Italian songs came from his experiences as a young man during the war – experiences that had stayed with him all his life. She remembered now that she had often heard him humming well-known Italian tunes in the house and smiled to hear from her uncle that he had embarrassed them all when they were boys by singing them very loudly outside, while mowing the lawn in careful stripes.

In her mind's eye, she saw again the smart, gentle man who had sat with her at their dining table in his favourite 'shades of toffee' checked shirt, brown tie, trousers and tidy cardigan with those big round buttons that seemed to her like hot cross buns. He had read dinosaur books with her as a young child. He had listened and commented as she chatted on, pointing things out to him in the book that he might not have noticed. She remembered how he had smiled and thanked her. Now she felt unsettled, even a little angry, burning with curiosity about the man she could no longer speak to. What was his connection with Italy? How had the Second World War taken him there? She was now hearing for the first time that his bond with that land, forged in war, had remained strong to his life's end. Why?

As if leaving her with a message, the closing music was his favourite Italian song, *Torna a Surriento*. She looked at the translation in the Order of Service. *Come back to Sorrento.*

Come back to Sorrento! It seemed to call to her as it sang its irreverent way around the pillars and to follow her as she stepped out of the small church, into the balmy warmth of the day.

The hearse left for the crematorium with only her Nanna accompanying it, for a quiet, personal, last goodbye alone. The remainder of the congregation, Reginald's family, elderly work colleagues, young cousins and neighbours, left the church quietly. As they made their way on foot along the lane to the nearby country pub for lunch, the brightness of the sun drove away the dark shadows of the service and soon the mourners chatted animatedly, glad to meet up, even if for a sad event.

Trays of buffet food came and went, glasses were filled and emptied, more visitors from Reg's past came to pay their respects and share their memories.

At last the hubbub began to fade, the party was thinning and the bar staff were beginning to tidy the tables.

It was then that the pub door was opened with a sudden, misjudged force that sent it banging against the back of a nearby chair. Every head turned. Everyone stopped talking. Beth looked over from a conversation with one of her cousins.

A young man in a dark suit with fair-ish hair and a narrow black tie stepped in before the returning door could swing back into the sunlit space it had so violently left. Glancing quickly from person to person, he seemed to be searching for someone in particular. Who was this stranger, wondered Beth, and why had he come to her grandfather's wake?

The funeral guests soon turned back to their conversations, assuming this interloper was there for a reason other than the wake, so it was Beth who went over to greet him.

'Hello, can I help you?' she asked kindly and he turned to face her.

'Ah! It could be you!' he said, scanning her awkwardly.

'Er, sorry?' Beth looked confused.

He flicked his dark blond hair back from his forehead with a twist of his head. His neck began to flush red at the collar. 'Are you – are you, by any chance – Beth?' he asked quickly.

'Yes, but I think you must be looking for my grandmother,' replied Beth calmly. 'This wake is for her husband, Reginald Selby.'

'No, no, it is Beth I am looking for,' he said staring intently at her and standing rather stiffly, one shoulder further forward than the other, as if embarrassed at being so sure.

'Then you have found her. I'm Beth,' she said.

Robert was relieved finally to be here, and especially to have found Beth. He had not had a good start to the day. All too early that morning, his phone had buzzed wildly, disturbing his deep sleep and interrupting a much-needed lie-in. He had stirred reluctantly and, head still on the pillow, had thrust out an arm, fumbling to grab the mobile from the bedside table and bring it to his half-open eyes. There was a new message, it read: 'Robert, have you remembered to take the suitcase to Reginald Selby's funeral? Dad.'

'Why does a message from my dad always sound like a telling off?' he frowned. Then, as he stretched and shivered himself awake, Robert realised what the message was about. 'Damn!' He *had* forgotten. Of course he had.

'Why do *I* have to go?' he complained to himself as he hurtled out of bed towards the shower. 'I don't even know the family!'

Despite all that, he had managed to arrive in time and had even delivered the suitcase to the right person.

Beth stood in front of him, smiling a little – unable to resist a touch of amusement at this young man's manner. She put out her hand for him to shake and he raised his with an enthusiastic jerk, only to realise that this hand still clutched a small suitcase, so he swapped the case to his other hand, which was holding his car keys. He dropped them with a clatter on the floor, whipped down his free hand at the end of a long arm to scoop them up, stuffed them into a pocket and finally extended a hand to take Beth's, which was still waiting patiently, mid-air.

He took a breath. 'Let me explain,' he said, realising that this had not quite gone smoothly so far. 'My name is Robert Palmer and my father is, I mean was, well still is really, your grandfather's solicitor, that is until his affairs are all sorted. Anyway, my father could not come today but wanted me to extend his condolences. I nearly forgot, so had to rush, but I'm here now. I'm a solicitor too, by the way. I work with my father.'

'Thank you,' said Beth, 'I see. Well, I think I see! But why to me and not my grandmother?'

'I mean I would like to extend condolences to you and your grandmother too.'

'Thank you. That's very kind.'

There was a pause. Robert smiled at Beth, apparently relieved. A few seconds passed.

'Was there something else?' enquired Beth.

'Ah yes! I also came because of this,' said Robert, raising up and presenting the small, brown leather suitcase, 'That's what it is about.' He held the small suitcase flat in both hands, like an offering. He smiled at her with the satisfaction of a mission completed.

Beth stared for a moment at him in surprise and then looked down at the suitcase as she took it from him. It was old, with reinforced corners, a stitched leather handle and the initials R.E.S. stamped in worn gold letters between the clasps. Its scuffed edges showed that it had been much used, but it was still sound, as if put aside at a certain point and kept for a special purpose. She turned to the solicitor with wondering eyes – 'But what... Why...?

'I don't know. But there's a letter for you too. Perhaps that explains its purpose. I'm sure it's important. My father says that Captain Selby was meticulous in his planning.' Robert smiled at her – a small encouraging smile.

'Again, that name – Captain Selby,' thought Beth. That purpose, whatever it was, seemed to have been passed to her.

The young solicitor's voice interrupted her thoughts and she looked up again. 'Here's the letter. Your grandfather wrote it several years ago in fact, so that there would be no confusion. That's how I knew that it had to be for you.' He took a simple white envelope from his inside jacket pocket and handed it to her. It was indeed addressed to her in her grandfather's recognisable handwriting. The sides were a little stretched, as if her name had been written on it and then more pages had been added than originally planned. She placed the suitcase on a nearby empty, round table and took the letter. It read 'To my dear granddaughter, Beth.'

'Here's my card,' added Robert, 'Call me if you need something, or if something isn't clear.' He held it out, but she was still focused on the envelope. Unsettled, he leaned uncomfortably to one side, as if unable to move his feet and slid it onto the small table next to the suitcase, adding unnecessarily, 'I probably won't know the answer, because I only recently qualified, but my dad will. Anyway, I'm happy to help.'

She, deep in thought, did not respond, but the conversation felt to him unfinished, so he added, perhaps with a little too much energy, 'Glad to have met you, Beth!' and extended his hand forcefully as if to underline the sentiment. Beth, distracted by the letter in her right hand, offered him her left to shake instead, which he did not know what to do with, so he patted it gently, then turned, embarrassed again, and hurried for the door. Beth looked up after him, not sure in that moment which was more confusing – the awkward young man, or the suitcase and letter he had brought.

Beth looked across to where her nanna was saying goodbye to some cousins and a couple of her husband's golfing friends. Beth waited until they had left the pub. Almost everyone had gone now, so she decided that she needed to ask her nanna about the case before walking out with it on this significant day in all their lives.

'Nanna?'

'Yes dear?'

'May I ask you something? Dadu's solicitor sent his son to deliver this to me today and I don't know anything about it.' She indicated the suitcase lying on the small, round bar table. 'He didn't say much, just gave me the case and a letter addressed to me from Dadu. He was keen to pass on his condolences to us, and of course from his father, Mr Palmer, but could not tell me any more about the suitcase. Do you know what's in it, Nanna?'

The widow, weary from the long day, looked across at the small, brown suitcase. She frowned and shook her head, as if searching for a memory, then walked over to the table and ran a well-manicured finger along the lid, tenderly. 'That's his old wartime suitcase. It was in the loft for a very long time. Reggie must have given it to his solicitor some years ago. I can't be sure what's in it or why he has passed it on to you, my dear. He shared some of his wartime experiences with me, but like most people after the war, there was probably more that he simply did not want to talk about. Just take it and have a look.' Her nanna patted Beth on the arm, then added, 'He was always very organised, so maybe the letter will explain. Perhaps there are some stories that he felt needed to be told – and if so, you should feel very touched that he has passed them on to you!' She started a smile, but it seemed too much effort and, resting one hand on the little table, sat down on the chair next to it with a sigh, as if signalling that there was nothing more to add. She looked suddenly exhausted and distracted, perhaps relieved that the sad event was finally over. 'Beth, I'm feeling very tired now. Your uncle is taking me home, so would you go and ask him if we can go now, please? I think I need a quiet cup of tea and a long rest. Thank you, dear.'

On the drive back to London in her Mini, her nanna's words kept returning. Were there stories that her Dadu needed to share? Why had he waited so long – in fact waited until she could no longer speak to him or ask him any questions? What was so difficult that it could only be revealed after the shadow of death had passed over and taken him with it? Her world seemed to have changed colour. The clear, bright light of that early morning, when she had set out for the funeral was now long gone. As she sped away along the dull, winding strip of endless road, the remaining daylight hung like a grey veil that filtered her memories of her grandad from her in a growing barrier of haze. Everything that was familiar now appeared further away. Beth's thoughts of sadness at losing her grandfather were mixed with a desire to pull back individual memories and examine them again and again. Were there hints or clues? Why were the Italian songs so important? She cast frequent glances in her rear-view mirror in the direction of the small brown suitcase lying on the back seat of the car. What had he held back? What was he sharing now? Why with her and what would the letter say?

Far from closing a chapter, this day had opened a whole new story.

2

The Letter

'There is history in all men's lives'
William Shakespeare, *Richard III*

Beth parked her car and climbed the stairs to her small, bright, rented flat, glad to enter its freshness and light after the long day. She looked around at the features that she had added to make it her own. The kitchen-diner walls were a summer sky-blue against which an artist friend had painted Ionic columns and artefacts from ancient Greece and Lycian Turkey. Her studies of classical literature, life, politics and art were not just a school topic, they were a passion she carried with her. Her grandfather had enjoyed Latin and Greek at school too, creating a link for her with the near and far-distant past. A pot plant and miniature orange tree combined with the light blue and white to frame the small room in the atmosphere of an eternal Mediterranean summer.

She dropped her car keys into her key tray – an ashtray replica of the Colosseum in Rome – and crossed to the bedroom. She put the suitcase down on the crisp pale yellow bedcover, and the contrast with the worn, brown-leather surface struck her. She felt separated from her Dadu by all the years that this long held possession represented, and yet the presence of the case in her room made him feel strangely close.

She felt a surge of emotion well up inside her and crease her face, so she involuntarily gulped a deep breath to steady herself. She stood for a moment to restore her usual calm composure, then kicked off her black high-heels decisively and exchanged her black suit for a loose T-shirt and leggings. In the kitchen, she drank a glass of water straight down and brought another back with her, putting it on the bedside table. It was almost dark, so she switched on the main light and bedside lamps, then sat on the edge of the bed. No. That did not feel right. She slid down the side of the cover to the floor, sitting on the pale, soft carpet. She pulled the suitcase gently down onto the floor next to her and placed the white envelope on top. She paused.

She looked again at the cracked gold letters R.E.S. on the case and ran her hand across the lid, hesitating for a moment midway, knowing he had touched that surface too. She picked up the envelope, noticing how it bulged slightly, as if the contents were restrained in a pocket slightly too small. She turned it over in her hands, hesitating to take the next step. Then, with an intake of breath she slipped a finger under the lightly closed seal flap and with a bold decisiveness he would have recognised in himself, opened it.

Frowning just a little and biting her lip in anticipation, she drew out several sheets of carefully folded handwritten paper. Reaching the centre sheet, she noticed, with a sudden sharp stab of emotion, that it had been written a few years ago. It must have been around the time his health began to decline. She seemed to hear his voice as she began to read her Dadu's familiar clear, unfussy and slightly spikey handwriting – such a contrast with her Nanna's florid hand! She smiled as she saw he had used his fountain pen. Naturally.

My dear Granddaughter, Beth,
I am writing to you as your dad drives you away in the car, after a lovely afternoon's visit. We did have fun making those dot to dot pictures together and looking at the story books, didn't we? I can still see you waving from the car window and grinning at me with that look that says, 'You and me, Grandad, we shared something today.' That is why I have decided to share this with you.

My memory is dying before the rest of me and I know that by the time you are old enough to hear and understand my story, I shall either be dead or no longer able to recall my tale. Dementia is robbing me slowly of all that I love, so I am entrusting this information to my lawyer for you to receive at my funeral, whenever that may be.

Beth paused, blinked her long lashes and a few involuntary tears rolled down her cheek. She leant across, grabbed a tissue to wipe them away. She took a deep breath and carried on reading.

This old suitcase contains tickets, notes, maps and plans that are the traces of my story. The events of my years serving in the army during the Second World War have stayed with me all my life. When you reach the age that I was then, I hope you will understand their significance.

Today, I saw in you the spark of interest in history – in our collective past and those who lived before us – that once I saw in myself, which is why, dear Beth, this is a story you should know. It is part of your history and perhaps you will be able to re-tell it for the family in a way that I felt I could not.

Beth's gaze lifted from the page and she stared, eyes again full of tears, at the darkening window of her room. She felt as if she was entering another time through the emptiness of the night. Impatient now to learn more, she put down the half-read letter and softly touched the old leather of the suitcase. She sighed and slowly pushed the two sliding locks to each side. They were stiff and resisted at first, then the fasteners clicked, flicked open. With her heart beating extra hard, she carefully lifted the lid, releasing the musty smell inside: old paper, stale loft and a puff of atmosphere from the past. She breathed in deeply this essence of a time long held captive and felt her heart beat even faster. Opening the case was like opening a doorway to a life and world she did not know. What would she find? Secrets that shock or surprise? Perhaps trauma and tragedy? She felt a knot in her stomach and her hand hovered for a moment over the fragile pages. Taking a deep breath, she delicately lifted the first document.

On the first sheet, the symbol of the Bedfordshire and Hertfordshire Regiment stood proud and, peeping out from underneath it, the yellowing paper of a sign-up document dated June 1940. Her grandad would then have been just 19.

Below it lay a photograph of him, Reg, as he was known as a young man. She recognised the faces of the family around him, his father Edward, sister Kathleen, stepmother and younger half-brother, Victor, aged perhaps about nine. Faded old black ink on the back told her that they were at the door of the Round House Lodge, Ware, Hertfordshire where Reg had lived as a child. Beth took in the image of a black and white timber-framed cottage near the grounds of a large estate, Fanhams Hall, where she later discovered his father Edward, her great-grandfather, had been Head Gardener.

Another picture was perhaps meant to show his parents arm in arm by the door, but by chance, it had caught the young Reg aged about 12, one hand placed on the gatepost, vaulting over it into the garden instead of opening the gate. His father's face was turned, mouth open to chastise, while his stepmother looked on, smiling at his youthful energy.

The papers were tied in bundles with red document tape, but they were collated by category rather than place or date – faded old maps here, dog-eared tickets there, letters and notes in the third batch.

She carefully untied the bundles and delicately lifted each page from its resting place, conscious that the last hand to touch these documents had been her grandad's. Feeling her interest and excitement mounting, she scanned the headings and turned each page to uncover more. Her eyes were bright now, sparkling with curiosity. She found dates and places, photographs and tickets, disparate documents that, pieced together, might create a timeline through an era of great significance in both Reg's own life, and indeed in global history.

She stopped suddenly, holding several sheets at once. 'Slow down!' she admonished herself. 'This is not the way.' She took a deep breath and looked across the fan of papers spread out over the floor. 'There's so much here. I need to be more systematic. More like Dadu,' she told herself. 'I need to arrange and catalogue them all in chronological order.' It was fully dark outside now, but Beth was too deeply immersed in this story to stop. As she worked, gradually the early papers fitted together to build a picture from the past.

After what seemed like no more than a moment, she saw that a couple of hours had passed. She got up and prepared a snack. Looking back at the papers, she realised that she needed to get her head around all this by recording what she had uncovered. She went over to her desk, put down her plate and half-eaten toast and slipped her laptop out of its case. Focusing on the blank new screen, she paused, like a marathon runner gathering strength before the start of a long and demanding, but exciting course, then typed: 'Reginald Edward Selby …'

Reginald Edward Selby, 1920–2005: Background from documents and notes

As she looked through the first documents, scraps of early memories returned to her, some passing comments that had meant nothing at the time, but which now were the patches of colour to combine with the papers in front of her to build a real, feeling, living picture of her grandfather as a young man.

Reg was in his early teens when he was signed up to the Officers' Training Corps by his father, Edward Selby, who had seen through the whole of World War I in the trenches. Now, in another war, Reg would be following in his father's footsteps. Those were large boots to fill, because Edward had won the Distinguished Service Medal in France in 1915 for rescuing a fallen comrade in no-man's land (the land between the trenches of the opposing sides), and being wounded by a bullet to the neck in the process. Beth found in Reg's handwritten papers an interesting note that, even as his son signed up for military service, it still rankled with Edward that he himself could not be given the Distinguished Service *Order* because he was not an officer. Although he held the senior non-commissioned officer rank of 'Platoon Serjeant', Beth discovered that Edward had always said that any son of his would be an officer, if not by birth then by study – and it was never too soon to start!

Edward Selby, DSM aged 23 years.
(Family archive)
845 Sjt. E. SELBY 1st Bn. TF

Citation
For conspicuous gallantry and efficiency displayed throughout the campaign, and particularly for much excellent work as Platoon Serjeant, when he frequently showed great courage and ability under heavy fire. (30.6.15)

Sergeants, 3/1st Hertfordshire Regiment, WWI. (Family archive)

Edward Selby, third row in the above photograph. (Family archive)

845 Sjt. E. SELBY 1st Bn. TF
For conspicuous gallantry and efficiency displayed throughout the campaign, and particularly for much excellent work as Platoon Serjeant, when he frequently showed great courage and ability under heavy fire. (30.6.15)

Edward Selby with eight medals. (Family archive)

Sifting through the old papers, Beth worked out that, when a state of war was declared for a second time in his life, in September 1939, Edward Selby was perhaps considered too old to serve outside the UK. This must have been why he volunteered for the local Home Guard. It became clear to Beth that Reg, son of a highly decorated war hero, and now 18 years of age, was expected to sign up to serve his country without delay. Reg duly joined the 70th Young Soldiers battalion. Academically, he had always been a strong student at school and did well in army training too, gaining a Certificate A qualification. The Hertfordshire Regiment may have been merged with the Bedfordshires, but his cap badge was the Hertfordshire hart. Beth read how this second generation soldier was soon a Lance Corporal and then quickly promoted to Corporal. Then by the following summer, he achieved part of his father's dream: he reached the rank of an officer, becoming Second Lieutenant in the Second Battalion, Bedfordshire and Hertfordshire Regiment. How proud Edward must have been!

But it was not only the official story that Beth was learning. There were lighter, much more human moments recorded in Reg's characteristic handwriting too. The man she called Dadu had written many notes. Amongst these she found an admission that, one unforgettable day in Glasgow, he had led a whole armoured convoy straight into a cul-de-sac! She smiled as she added this incident to her typed document. Thirty-five army vehicles had had to reverse and re-route! She read how, unsurprisingly, he never lived this down amongst the lads. But she also read how, as a response, Reg took to memorising as much detail as possible on any maps he could lay his hands on. He spent long evenings preparing for each possible new manoeuvre, trying to envisage the landscapes in his mind that these documents represented. He quickly developed an innate sense of landscape and direction. In the weeks following, repeat practice on manoeuvres honed his natural ability to see the landscape laid out like a map in his head – which would prove invaluable in the months and years ahead. But it would only be when, many months later, she came across details in other documents, that she would finally discover how absolutely vital this episode involving the cul-de-sac had turned out to be.

Beth stopped typing for a moment and laid down Dadu's notes. She thought about things he had said to her, encouraging her to learn as much as possible and take opportunities when they presented themselves. She felt she could hear Dadu's calm, clear voice, full of warmth for her. From everything she was learning about Dadu's own father, it seemed as if Great-Grandad Edward might have said the same. She created for herself the conversations father and son may have had as

Two generations, two World Wars, father and son. (Family Archive)

Reg moved from training camp to training camp. She could imagine Reg repeat-edly hearing his father's voice in his head, 'I'm proud of you, Son. An officer in the family! But remember that with authority goes responsibility. Lead from the front, keep a cool head and always prepare yourself. The challenges you face may be unknown as yet, but if you have skills, you can find a way through.'

It seemed to Beth that those words – or words very much like them – must have been constantly echoing in Reg's ears, since the papers showed that he had clearly taken the chance to follow every training course he possibly could. These were based mainly in Scotland or the border areas and included: GHQ Battle School; Street Fighting Course; Physical Training Instructors Course; Army Gas School and an Assault Engineering Course.

By the end of 1942, it was time for the many hard hours of tough training to be put to the test. Reg had moved all around the country on these postings – from guarding aerodromes at Cranfield in Buckinghamshire and at Duxford, Cambridgeshire to exercises at the Barony Estate, Parkgate, Dumfriesshire, Scotland. His notes spoke of nights of assault landing practice around Inveraray, Argyllshire. There, as an officer, he had to lead the way in the pitch black over the side of the ship, down the scramble-net onto the assault landing craft, from which he would leap first into the freezing shallows and lead the men up the cliffs and inland to the target location. These challenges were a far cry from his earlier experiences with an officer cadet training unit at Barmouth. The orders here were simply to march into cold, choppy Welsh waters, where, once waist-deep in the brine, the fearsome sergeant major appeared to enjoy issuing the order to, 'mark time'. All the drills would show their value in the months and years ahead.

Before his twenty-second birthday, he was Lieutenant in command of Number One Platoon, C Company, 2nd Battalion, Bedfordshire and Hertfordshire Regiment and deemed ready to be deployed. Where would they have to go?

The answer came all too soon – North Africa.

Deployment. In wartime. How did that feel? To Beth who had grown up in a land that had been at peace for many decades, the very thought was terrifying. Africa? Back then, how exotic, strange, wild and unknown must that have been to a lad from Hertfordshire who had never so much as been across the Channel. Another continent! In the modern world brimming with information about almost everything and everywhere at the tap of a finger, it is difficult to understand how little the embarking soldiers would have known about their destination. The bare, official facts of departure were there in front of her – old black type on old, discoloured paper. She picked up the piece of paper and felt her fingers quiver, as if a shiver of the fear and anticipation that those soldiers may have felt had reached her too. Was there more here about that day, that journey? Perhaps a journal or comment? Then she noticed some faint scribbles, sometimes in pencil, in tiny handwriting on the back of a small, brown, used envelope. She found snatches of recorded moments, quickly jotted down, so as not to be forgotten. Here was his voice speaking directly to her across the decades. Beyond the formal notices in the suitcase, here were glimpses of her grandfather's personal journey.

The background facts no longer felt to her like history. Here was her old and wrinkled, gently smiling Dadu as a young, strong man. He, like her now, was only in his early twenties with his life ahead of him, facing the reality that this may all be about to change. She set aside her laptop and felt her throat tighten as she connected with the emotions behind the words on the papers that lay before her. She stood up and shivered involuntarily as she looked out of the window, up at the darkness of the night sky. In her mind, she tried to join him on that first journey into unimaginable danger.

3

Africa

All our efforts to form a front in the Balkans were founded upon
the sure maintenance of the Desert Flank in North Africa.
Winston Churchill,
The Second World War, volume III: the Grand Alliance

As Reg's ship set off from Garston Dock, Liverpool in December 1942, heading out to join a fleet in the Straits of Gibraltar, he could never have imagined what would follow.

The Straits were a key access point for the Allies to the Mediterranean Sea, but were hard to defend. The narrowness of this stretch of water made the large convoy an easy target as it passed through. As night brought the cover of darkness for enemy planes, their aircraft drew in to attack. A pale moon painted bright strokes of light onto the ships as they cut through the dark blue shimmering waves. It seemed to mark them out for the approaching gunners. Soon the peaceful, starry night sky was scorched with bursts of fire, as shells fell onto the ships, exploding men and metal out and across the restless waters. Bombs hit or missed their slow-moving targets with the apparent randomness of devilish chance. Machine guns rattled all around and Reg could only watch, face rigidly set into an angry frown, knuckles stark white, as he gripped the guardrail. Troopship after troopship sank into darkness, leaving the screaming injured and the silent dead tossed to and fro by the cold, emotionless sea.

On Reg's ship, the captain gave the order to plough on to their destination as fast as the engines would allow. Their task was to get through alive. Reg and his men stood huddled in groups on deck watching the sickening success of the bombers. With every screeching bomb that dropped, every blast that sounded and each new wave of screams, they shivered – willing, desperate, but completely unable to help. And fearful too for themselves. Behind them, beyond the churning wake of their ship, survivors struggling to stay afloat, many unable to swim, were abandoned to hold on, somehow, until the planes had gone and rescue boats could be sent to find them.

Reg searched his memory for verses in the Bible calling for mercy for these men in their extreme distress from his many hours in church with his family. Then the hairs on the back of Reg's neck rose up and his eyes stung with repressed tears, as the spontaneous singing of the seafarer's hymn, *Eternal Father, strong to save*, drifted across the waves around him from ship to ship and from man to man. As if hearing his father's voice in his head, 'Lead from the front…' he cleared his throat to lead his company from the next verse, shakily at first. Then, calling on his years as head choir boy in the small church back home in Ware, he took a deep breath, raised his voice and sang out the sombre chorus…

O hear us when we cry to Thee,
For those in peril on the sea…

At this moment, Reg wished he had insisted his father tell him more about *his* war. His eyes darted back and forth, picking out the agonised moonlit faces and desperate raised arms as they became distant dots in the water, and then quickly faded into the shadows of the waves. He began to realise that it was not physical training and army rules that would count here, but how you handle the horror of the scenes witnessed, the fear for yourself, and then the guilt of survival. His father must have felt all of these things many, many times. When the last notes of the hymn floated out to the abandoned men in the water, he clenched his jaw and swallowed hard, as if to push his feelings back down his throat. But he determined, there on the deck, fists clenched, to remember these emotions and hold the feelings of fury, frustration, fear and sorrow as a benchmark for what may lie ahead.

The ships that survived the merciless bombing that night and got through the narrow passage sailed on, to land in Algiers in early January 1943. Reg and his company of fellow soldiers gratefully filed off the ship and clambered up the stone steps at the dockside onto dry land. Dry indeed it was. Desert ground and almost unabating sun. Winter here felt like late spring at home, with temperatures of over 60 degrees Fahrenheit – 16-plus degrees Celsius. A little rain now and then meant there were occasional patches of scrubby greenery, but the blooming, verdant gardens of Hertfordshire were a world away.

Tough fighting in the increasing heat along the Mediterranean coast of North Africa in Tunisia awaited C Company, as they were engaged in supporting the effort to complete a pincer movement against Rommel's *Afrika Korps*. However, the odds were stacked against them. British and Allied ships were sailing in haste to destinations on the North African coastline, which was dominated by the troops and strong reputation of leading German general, Erwin Rommel. He was by now well established and, as Winston Churchill said, a 'very daring and skilful opponent.'

C Company struggled to hold on, while the Allies' Eighth Army was sent to answer the advances of the German and Italian campaigns. Success here was crucial to the Allied plan, so infantrymen were drawn from across the British Empire, with varying levels of training and a wide range of cultural backgrounds to make up a large, disparate, body of fighting men.

For Reg and the other freshly arriving forces, still with the images of drowning sailors stark in their minds, the constant risks of war quickly became very real. Reg and the men rested by day and set out on foot at night – at times enduring up to five days and nights without sleep. Some night missions were for reconnaissance, others were targeted raids in fighting patrols. These were the most dangerous, as the forays could meet with an all-out counter-attack from the enemy.

The threat of death hovered over them like the terrifying sword of Damocles, suspended by just one horse's hair, to fall at random and cut down whoever was beneath it. The very first casualty was the commanding officer in charge of the newly arrived units, killed by a shell. Rank, it seemed, was no protection from the arbitrary and devastating destruction of war. Individuals could do little to increase their chances of surviving unharmed – that was out of their hands. All they could do was to take a few measures to reduce their chances of dying. Darkness would at least provide some cover, so operating at night whenever possible was a simple protection they could adopt.

Over the coming weeks and months, Reg held his nerve as men around him were injured and sent home. Then, one night his steely nerve was almost broken. The unit was manning a position away from the camp, monitoring it for enemy activity. Reg was standing guard with his runner, Private Wells. The myriad of stars in the vastness of the North African sky could do little to light the moonless night and they stared sightless into the blackness, listening intently. There was not a sound in the chill desert air. Somewhere out in the darkness a rifleman raised the muzzle of his weapon and levelled the sights to his eye with practised accuracy. He picked his target and took careful aim. A shot rang out. Reg turned his own gun in the direction of the gunshot, about to retaliate, when a rasping sound came from Wells and Reg caught his falling, bloodied body in his arms. As return fire from his men rattled towards the enemy marksman, Reg tried to raise Wells's slumped figure to see his face in the dark, looking for signs of life.

But the colour and life was fast draining from his companion. Instead of fear or sorrow Reg felt rage rise up inside him, a fury so fierce it exploded the boundaries of any feelings he had experienced till then. The veins throbbed in his head and his jaw locked. A surge of emotion roared silently out of his burning lungs and into the night. This pain outstripped the desperate sadness, the total helplessness he had felt on the ship. He silently yelled at the Gods for their injustice. He held Wells's body close, as if to protect him, pointless as that now was, then lifted him in his arms and carried him away from the firing positions, laying him gently and reverently down.

As he ran a fevered, shaking hand through his dark blond hair and stared at his inert friend, guilt stepped in. Why Wells? Why not him? How could this deliberate act of destruction happen right next to him? How could he have let this happen, yet how could he have prevented it?

Then the voice of his sergeant major intruded gently but firmly, 'Leave the silent ones, Sir. They are already with the angels. Only the living scream.' Reg looked up, angry at first, but then, suddenly became conscious of the muffled cries of other injured men. He nodded to his sergeant major, grateful for the reminder. 'Keep a cool head,' echoed a voice from somewhere deep inside. Lieutenant Selby saluted his fallen compatriot and said a quiet prayer, while waiting comrades stood by to wrap the body, ready to transport it back to base camp.

Reg strode back to his fighting men and glared into the dark, breathing deeply to steady his racing mind. His father's face seemed to turn and look at him from the shadows out in the dusty terrain in front of them and nod in solemn acknowledgement. Were these feelings echoes of the anger and pain his father had felt in the trenches, now rippling through time to the new war? The son was starting to understand the silence of his father, keeping his furies, wrought in the furnace of the fight, contained and locked away in his gruesome war chest. As Reg stood scanning the dark landscape, every nerve alert, weapon raised, inwardly he dug a secret place in his soul and began to bury in it his own ugly trove.

⁎ — ⁎

Beth stood up, as if to shake off the unwelcome images and paced across the room to the kitchen. Then, remembering that she had a glass of water in the bedroom, returned and took a sip. Her tidy room and carefully chosen decorations reassured her. That museum poster of Hadrian's famous statue. Her well-thumbed copy of *The Odyssey* – her Dadu had studied Greek and Latin at school too – he would have known its stories. She drank the rest of the water just staring at its cover, her mind wandering through those pages filled with conflict, enemy lands, bloodshed and... Putting down the glass, she chased from her mind the uncomfortable parallels with the twentieth century tale unfolding before her. Carefully, she set the early items from inside the suitcase aside and knelt to pick up a piece of thin, folded, yellowing paper. As any kind of paper was no doubt in short supply, Reg seemed to have made notes for his reports on whatever scraps he could find.

With nervous fingers, she opened it and new scenes, held wrapped in these pages for so long, flashed into the light.

R. E. Selby in North Africa. (Family archive)

Unit photograph, North Africa. (Family archive)

Struggling to read the cramped, tiny handwriting, she learnt how, on 14 April 1943, Number 1 Platoon of C Company and Number 1 Platoon of D Company were ordered to occupy the high forward ridges of the mountainous terrain to cover the advance of the rest of the brigade through a valley between high Tunisian ranges. The 'intel' was that there was no risk of an air attack, as the Luftwaffe was believed to be on reconnaissance elsewhere, so the task was to protect brigade troops passing through on the ground from ambush by enemy troops. This also meant that the spitfires which Reg had seen win so many of the dog fights in other skirmishes since his arrival here would not be called on to protect them that day.

The night was beginning to fade into a sullen grey pre-dawn as the men climbed up the steep, uneven slopes, picking their way past boulders on slippery, crumbling shale underfoot. Up, up to meet the first streaks of dawn in the cloudless sky at the top of the ridge. The ridge itself jutted up into the sky, an ancient and uneven serrated jaw crowning the escarpment in myriad angles of solid rock. The officers told the men in each platoon to look around for cover, but there were no trees, no earthy banks, there was nowhere to dig in. They found places to lie flat between the rocks, or they crouched behind boulders and pointed their weapons out and down. Some slid into the shadows of narrow crevices, ready to fire on any enemy that might appear below.

They had been in position barely a few moments when a distant buzz drifted towards them in the warming air. Reg called for quiet and the company listened in disbelief as the familiar drone of enemy aircraft engines steadily advancing across the clear skies got louder with each passing second. This should not be happening! He squinted at the sky, seeking out the tell-tale dark specks that signalled the imminent arrival of this unexpected threat. Enemy planes were almost overhead.

At that moment, a new, closer sound caught the air and he darted his gaze hastily along the ridge. The regular crunch of fast-moving boots on dry rocks was clear and getting louder. It had to be German ground forces, though they were not expected to be in the area either. They must be planning to ambush the very column that C and D Company were there to protect. Attack from above and attack from the ground seemed imminent. There was no time to react.

The Germans had indeed spotted the arrival of the Allied men and realised they had to eliminate this defence force, if their planned attack on the troops about to arrive in the valley below could be a success. With the bonus of protection from the approaching air cover overhead, the German commander now gave the order to throw grenades towards the two Allied companies and be ready to move forward along the ridge to take control of it as soon as the planes had strafed it with gunfire.

Amid the rattle of enemy guns, C and D Company commanders barked orders to their men in quick succession, 'Take cover! Take cover!' Within seconds, grenades and shells exploded all around the exposed British soldiers, sending slices of rock whipping in all directions. The vicious rock-shards speared the men where they stood or pierced their backs where they lay.

As Reg shouted to his men, something whizzed across his peripheral vision – a grenade – falling beside him amongst the boulders. Instantly, and automatically, he placed his palm on the biggest rock at his side and hand-vaulted over it, landing crouched in the dusty ground the other side. The grenade exploded and a spray of deadly splinters shot in all directions, but Reg pressed his back against the solid rock and, sheltered under its slight overhang, pulled his knees in tight to his chest, so that the daggers of rock fell harmlessly past him, clattering on the rough ground.

Pulling himself back out and shaking off some smaller shards, he quickly scanned the scene. Men – many of them his men – were lying sprawled and motionless or screaming in agony, bloodied and torn amongst the rocky boulders. As his mind raced to find the right orders to shout in the chaos of this horror, the words of his sergeant major repeated in his head, 'Leave the silent ones. They are already with the angels. Only the living scream.'

With so many voices echoing cries of pain across the ridge, he called out a few words of comfort. 'Breathe slowly and hold your nerve. We'll get to you as soon as we can!' He looked around for other able-bodied men to direct, but barely anyone was on their feet. Lieutenant Selby shuddered involuntarily. The raised arms of the injured men calling for his help reminded him of the many stranded sailors calling and waving helplessly in the sea, as their ships were bombed off Gibraltar.

The enemy planes were circling round to return and strike again. There was no way to fight back, and how could he manage an orderly retreat down the steep, rocky ridge with so few men able to sit up, let alone stand? How could the injured be protected? He called to two men to move the least hurt to whatever cover they could find, but his words were drowned out by foreign battle cries. He watched in disbelief as enemy soldiers appeared across the ridge – heads down, weapons raised, charging towards them. In what seemed like a few seconds, their position was overrun by the advancing German troops, taking quick advantage of the chaos that the grenades, gunfire and shells had caused. The German officer in charge was shouting orders and signalling directions with his pistol. Reg watched in horror as D Company platoon commander, who was still calling orders to his men further ahead on the ridge, was shot dead where he stood.

Then a small detachment from the German force was despatched to look for trophy officers to take prisoner. Major Young and Lieutenant Selby were grabbed and led away. Now there was nothing they could do to help their injured men or recover the dead.

Hands bound, they were led down to German trucks, stumbling over the stony ground as dawn rays were swallowed by the glare of the full, white sunlight that seeped over the horizon sweeping away shade and colour before it. Reg looked across the rough road to see if he could catch a glimpse of any survivors from his company and saw some of the men with blooded backs being slung face-down over donkeys, some calling out in pain, others too injured to protest. Reg could see the dark red streaks on their uniforms, where the pieces of shrapnel and shards of rock had lodged in their spines and buttocks. They were led away in a macabre procession. A few men from the lower ranks, who could still walk were tied together and prodded to follow behind. Where would they be taken? Would their wounds be properly treated? Would Reg ever see any of them again? He clenched his bound fists, straining against the bonds – he was once again power-less to help. The butt of a German rifle pushed him roughly forward to climb into the back of the waiting truck.

The convoy headed for Tunis, where the lorries at last stopped at what seemed like the enemy headquarters, based in a single-storey former warehouse building. The prisoners were marched inside by armed guards.

One by one, the captives, British officers, were led into an interrogation room. When Reg entered the small office, across the desk sat an impeccably presented German officer writing with a smart ink pen. The guard prodded Reg to speak. He cleared the desert dryness from his throat and stated his name, rank and number. 'Reginald Selby, Lieutenant, 5955945.'

The officer across the desk looked up and sighed, disappointed. He put down the pen, leant back in his chair and began a conversation as if they were sitting together in a café off the Burlington Arcade. 'You know, I like London. I lived there before the war. The culture is very … infectious, yes. It draws you in! I even became a football fan! I was a great supporter of Arsenal Football Club – would you believe that!' he added with a brief chuckle. His English was immaculate.

He lit a cigarette and shook his head. 'England and Germany should never be enemies, Lieutenant Selby. We have too much in common. We are too alike. Both smart, both hard-working – we both like beer and football! This is really a great shame. A great shame.'

He rested the cigarette on the small metal ashtray. 'Can I tempt you to talk to me?' he asked, interlacing his fingers and resting his hands on the desk as he leant forward, raising his eyebrows, then dropping them and relaxing his face into a smile. 'I would like that very much!'

Reg replied again, 'Reginald Selby, Lieutenant, 5955945.'

'Very well. Very well. I see you are in no mood for a conversation. Pity. You are in uniform, so are officially a prisoner of war. You will be transported to Italy, not Germany unfortunately, because the Italians are still, for the moment, considered in overall command in North Africa.' He waved a dismissive hand in the air, then continued, 'It's not our choice but was agreed due to their military campaigns here before the start of our war. Hardly appropriate now, but there it is. Do you speak Italian?'

'Reginald Selby, Lieutenant, 5955945.'

Irritated, the interrogator stiffened his jaw and picked up his pen to resume writing. 'I would say, enjoy the culture and food there, but I understand that the prisoners receive very little of either. Goodbye, Lieutenant Selby. Next!'

⁂

In her quiet room, Beth paused, taking in the implications of what she had read. 'Dadu, oh Dadu!' In old films, these interrogation scenes were always a touch glamorous, the defiance of the soldier in the face of the enemy, and so on. But to experience it, not knowing what the outcome would be, how did that feel? They must have wondered if the rules of war would be respected of if they were going to be summarily shot after interrogation. Or were they going to be tortured? How strange and macabre it must have felt when the enemy across the desk had been a London resident joining other football supporters for a pint in the local pub only a short time before.

She straightened her back, relaxed her shoulders and rolled her stiff neck from side to side. Time for a break. She stood up and walked energetically to the kitchen to fetch a hot drink. While the kettle boiled, she stared mindlessly out of the window at buildings opposite. Some lights were still on, peeping from behind pulled curtains. In other windows, the rooms were dark but for the flickering images from a TV screen dancing on the blank ceilings she could see from her flat. Everything seemed calm, normal, routine. It was like waking in your safe, comfortable room from a nightmare that still hovers behind your eyes.

She went back to the bedroom with her drink, picked up her laptop and moved to the table. She sat down purposefully as if changing her own place in order to set about capturing his new location. She started to type: 'Italy,' to which she soon added the words 'prisoner of war'.

4

Prisoner of War, Italy

Italia! Oh Italia, thou who hast
The fatal gift of beauty which became
A funeral dower of present woes and past,
On thy sweet brow is sorrow plough'd by shame,
And annals graved in characters of flame.

Lord George Gordon Byron, (1788–1824),
Childe Harold's Pilgrimage, IV.370

The irony of hearing RAF fighter planes roaring overhead and wishing their bombs to miss, was not lost on Reg and the other POWs (Prisoners of War) as they were shipped out of North Africa across the wide Mediterranean. They travelled with a large group of other Allied POWs to Sicily, and then on to Naples in a stinking, rat-infested hold. They knew that other German ships transporting POWs had been bombed and sunk. Hundreds of men had been drowned that way, since the Allied air forces did not know who or what was on board. So it was a curious relief when, after what may have been several days at sea, they finally reached the POW camp in Naples on the west coast of Italy, Number *PG (Campo di Prigionieri di Guerra) 66, PM 3400.*

In terms of sanitation or comfort, the camp was not much of an improvement on the ship. Dysentery was rife and the camp was infested with flies. Men in dusty uniforms lay or sat around, ill and weak. The Officers' Mess was almost as much of a 'mess' as anywhere else. Reg and a few other officers from the boat were directed to a shabby building where they entered a simply-painted room with a few wooden chairs. A number of men, perhaps a dozen, were sitting around, some on the chairs, the rest on the floor. Those who had cigarettes smoked. Most looked dulled, perhaps a front to hide their fears or a retreat into passivity as a defence against the gnaw of hunger and emptiness of the long hours.

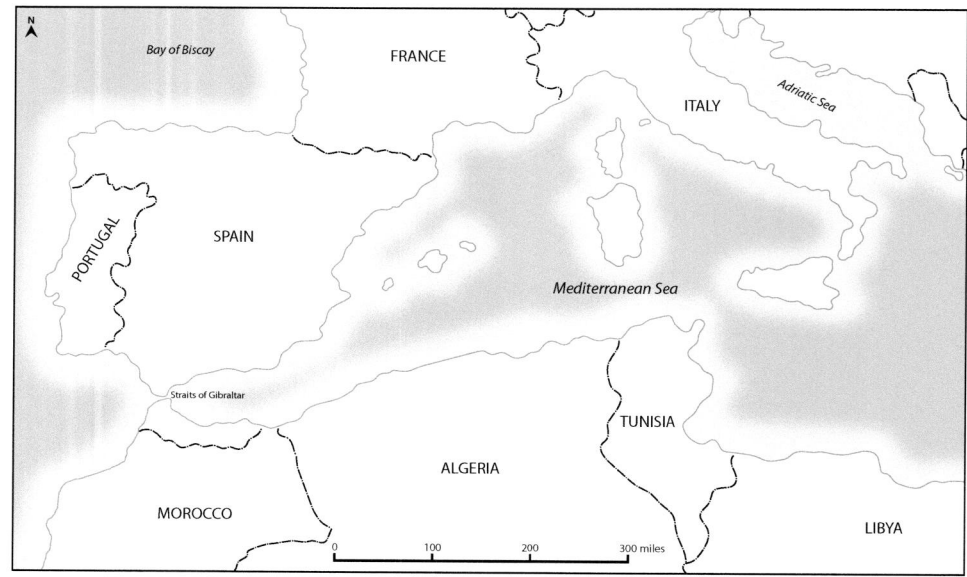

The Mediterranean showing North Africa and Italy.

Then a bold and energetic voice broke into the heavy atmosphere, 'Ah! New blood for our meagre gang, I see!' This was Lieutenant Norton Knatchbull from the Grenadier Guards, who was occupying one of the chairs, flanked by two comrades in arms. He was slightly injured, but otherwise appeared spirited enough.

'Blood and bone but very little meat!' replied Reg bitterly, feeling his stomach complain yet again. He gave a wry smile, then introduced himself. 'Lieutenant Reginald Selby, Bedfordshire and Hertfordshire 2nd Regiment. Captured in North Africa and fresh, or not in fact so fresh, from a stinking Nazi POW ship that brought us here to Naples.'

'It's pretty stinking around here too, so welcome, Selby. Selby – yes – that name's on the list. You're billeted to my hut. Listen, there are other ranks around. Find a few shillings a month and we'll sort out a batman who can soon get you set up.'

This chap behaved with natural authority. Reg could see that Norton was treated differently from other Lieutenants by the rest of the men too. He had noticed this in units before and assumed that Norton must be an officer from a titled family. He was right. The young man held the title Baron Brabourne, which explained his serving in the Guards.

One of the other men left his seat to act on the suggestion of finding a batman for the newly arrived officer and Norton signalled to Reg to take the now-vacant chair. Reg explained how C and D Company had been ambushed on the ridge and that the toll on the troops had been high. Most had gone to the hospital or morgue rather than the transportation truck.

'How was your interrogation?' continued Norton. More of the officers were gathering round, leaning in to listen.

'Not bad. The German officer wasn't a Nazi, just regular army. He was pro-British, and not looking to make an example of any of us. More than anything, he wanted a chat in English, but the conversation was rather one-sided as he only got name, rank and number from me!' A murmur of approval ran round the room and some of the other officers nodded as if they had done the same, including Norton.

'He still wanted to talk, so he told me about himself instead. He had lived in London before the war – and he even had the cheek to say that he supported Arsenal!' continued Selby.

'Ha! Pity that I wasn't there,' said Norton with a twinkle in his eye, taking a slow drag on his newly lit cigarette.

'Why's that?'

'You see, Reg, old boy,' he said, adjusting his position in his chair and swinging one leg up grandly to rest on the other knee, 'I'm a director of the Club!'

A ripple of laughter ran across the hungry, tired men, nourishing them with a much-needed sense of camaraderie, as Norton's directorship trumped the German's claim to be a supporter of *their* Arsenal Club. Reg jumped on the chance to connect. 'Ha! Yes! The interrogator was just an Arrrrs-enal!' at which the room replied, to a man, 'Gunners!' and mimed cocking a rifle. They all laughed again. It was the first social warmth Reg had felt since he had been taken captive.

In the coming days, Reg fitted in well. Whenever the atmosphere felt tense as men argued over food or clean socks, he used his interrogation tale to lighten the mood, like a signal. If language between the men became colourful, he would break across it with a loud call of 'Arrrrs-enal!' triggering the now obligatory response, 'Gunners!'

The POW camp was already overcrowded, but new truckloads of captured Allied soldiers were arriving almost daily, so men were being transported away in batches as soon as possible. They were being moved to other locations around Italy to free up space. Reg had heard that, among other potential destinations, a recently completed building near Parma was being converted into a camp, mainly for officers. Sure enough Reg became part of the contingent assigned for transfer there, though Major Young was not. Loaded again into trunks, they spent long hours bumping uncomfortably northwards through the hills, valleys, towns and hamlets of Italy to a small village called Fontanellato on the plains of Emilia-Romagna, over 400 miles north-east of Naples. At last, the vehicles swung in through metal gates that were locked behind them.

Rumour had it that the large, brick buildings originally built for religious orders had been redesigned to house the illegitimate children of Nazi officers in an orphanage that would educate them in the ways of the 'master race' to come. But for now, the space was needed to contain the ragged crew of captured military men, who were duly installed and guarded by Italian regular soldiers.

It was springtime and the days were getting warmer. From the camp, the inmates could see that the trees had regrown their plumage of bright greens and yellows and how the young leaves wafted gently in the April breezes. Spring flowers brightened the gardens and early blossoms decorated the meadows while the shoots of new crops in surrounding fields restored a sense of renewal to this landscape at war.

The facilities at *Campo Concentramento PG 49, PM 3200*, were basic, yet a great improvement on Naples. Over time, they found out that the site, set up by the Dominican Order of Preachers, had three parts in three separate buildings: one for the Order itself; another for the nunnery that became the laundry service for the inmates, but was originally the Sanctuary of the Blessed Virgin of the Sacred Rosary of Fontanellato; and a third building which was indeed intended to be an orphanage – the National Orphanage of the Madonna of Fontanellato.

This last became home to the 500 or so mainly British Army and RAF officers and some men of lower ranks who were to be transferred there over following months. The men had been captured in many different circumstances and each had a story to tell. Some were slightly injured in body, but most were emotionally scarred by what they had seen and experienced. All were worried about their families back home. Reg knew the drill. If no bodies were found, a telegram was sent to the families just saying 'Missing in Action.' 'The telegram should arrive about now,' he thought to himself and felt his gut wrench as he saw in his mind his father, stepmother and sister, anguish and worry falling across their faces as they read it, like the shadows of a lowered veil. As the eldest son, he felt a powerful responsibility to his parents and siblings, to support and protect them. Anticipating their distress was one of the hardest pains of his captivity to bear.

A faded telegram caught Beth's eye.

Dated 16 May 1943, it read:

> Deeply regret to inform you that your son, Lieutenant Selby R. E., Personal number 197146, Army number 5955945, is missing in action, after an encounter with the enemy on 14 April 1943. Please accept my most profound sympathies pending further news.

She tried to imagine the family and the enormity of the impact this news must have had on them. How difficult, how desperately unsettling, the three words must have been for his sister and parents: 'Missing in action.' Not to know if he was alive or dead. Not to know whether to hope or to grieve. Not to know if they would ever see their Reg again.

She looked back at the family photo at the front door of the black and white half-timbered Round House Lodge in sleepy springtime Hertfordshire. Images must have flashed through their minds of Reg lying dead on the sands of Tunisia, injured beyond recovery in a field hospital somewhere or beaten and tortured in an enemy cell. Even to hear that he was in a harsh wartime POW camp in Emilia-Romagna would have brought light to their darkness. But they knew nothing of POW camps in Italy. They only had the stark, typed message on the flimsy telegram.

She tried to imagine how the family must have felt. In the photo, the blossom on the cherry tree was coming into bloom above the last of the tulips swaying their ruby cups in the gentle breeze along the path to the front door. But there was no Reg to come vaulting over the garden wall.

Her imagination strayed to the family gathering for breakfast around the scrubbed wooden kitchen table. Edward Selby ready for the day's work in his gardening uniform, sister Kathleen cutting the bread in her white apron, half-brother Victor running to get to the table before he is declared late, and Reg's stepmother holding the teapot lid in place while pouring tea into each ready cup. Familiar sounds – the postman's hand on the gate latch and tread on the path, the ticking of the grandmother clock on the wall. But instead of letters posted through the letterbox, there's a knock at the door. Edward gets up to answer it. It is not the usual postman. By the door is the young telegram runner in uniform and cap, delivering telegrams on the first of his three daily rounds.

'Mr Edward Selby?' he asks, looking up at the stern man. 'Indeed,' replies Sergeant Major Selby, Home Guard. He glances down at the outstretched

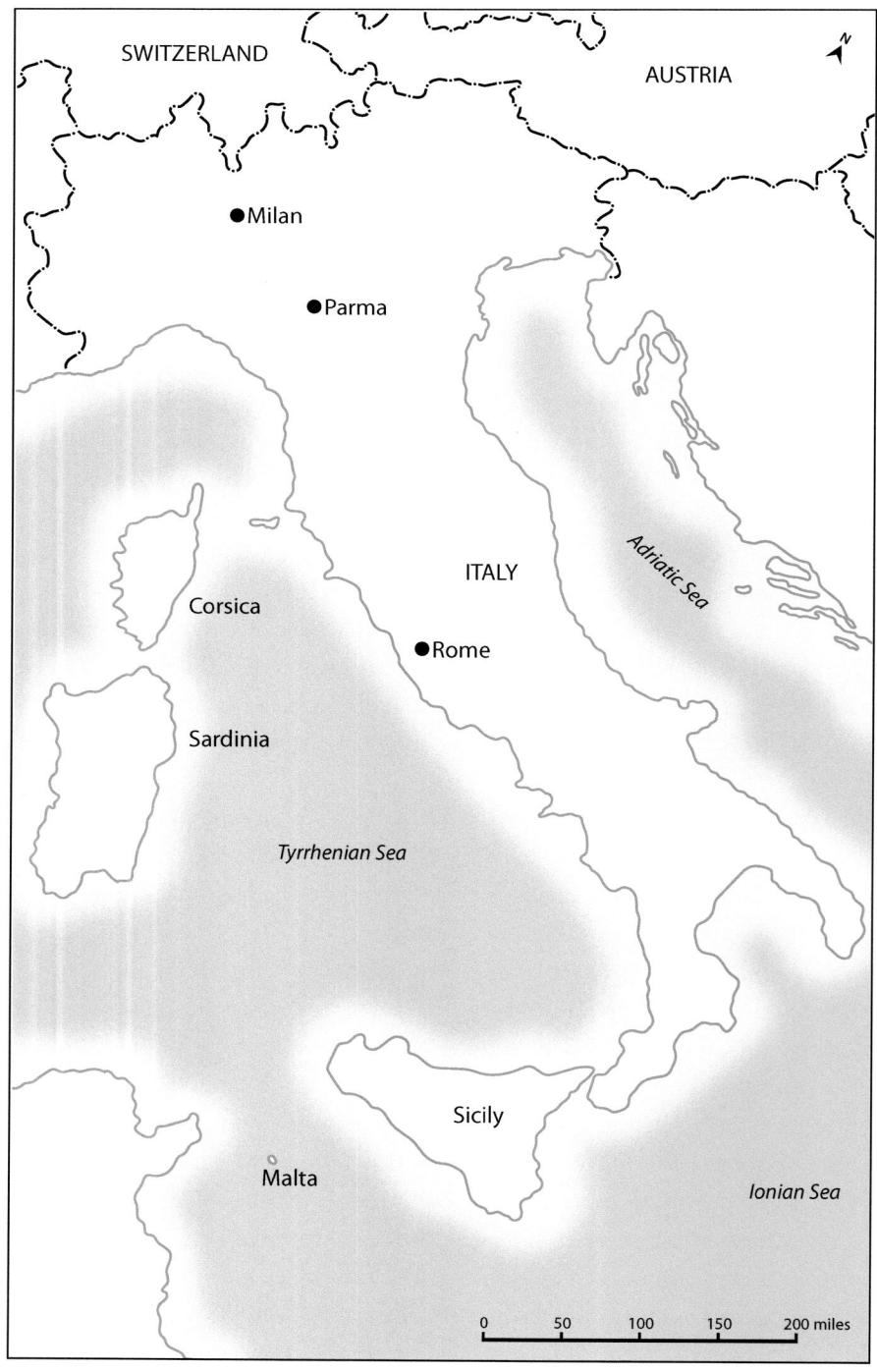

Italy showing Naples and Parma, Rome and Milan.

telegram. His face stiffens and the colour drains from his face. Lines around his mouth deepen as his lips tighten and turn down and he takes the telegram from the boy. 'No reply,' he barks, turning back into the house. The boy quickly touches his cap and runs for the gate. In his haste, he does not shut it properly. The former sergeant major looks back and narrows his eyes. '<u>Close</u> it!' he barks, like an order. The boy scrambles back and clicks the latch correctly, before sprinting away and past the hedge. He jumps on his bike and pedals madly in his haste to get out of sight.

In the doorway Edward stands rigid, looking down at the paper in his hand. He feels a gentle touch on his arm. His wife is beside him, looking at the sealed telegram. They stare at it, too shocked to move.

A voice from behind them calls in a tremulous tone, 'Father, what is it? What does it say?' Kathleen walks slowly to join them and Mr Selby pulls the lightly glued seal, which gives way and opens the thin paper to show the text within. He starts to read aloud but his voice cracks and he, not wanting to show his feelings, pushes the thin paper into his daughter's hands.

'Missing,' she reads. 'It just says missing, Father. Not dead. Not injured, just missing.' He stands squarely, eyes fixed on the floor. He hesitates for a moment, then gathers himself, picks up his thick gloves and leaves the house for work.

Young Victor at the table feels the emotion in the air and is desperate to break the long silence that follows. 'Bet he's hiding somewhere. My big brother was always good at that!' Then, seeing the tears filling his sister's eyes, realises that this is no time for joking and adds softly, 'He'll be alright, Kath. After all those practice manoeuvres without maps, if anyone can find his way home, it's our Reg!'

⌐ — ⌐

A few days later, when Beth opened up her laptop again, her thoughts turned back to the camp in Italy. From the papers in the suitcase she realised that the captured men had certain features in common. They were chiefly officers who had all been given some form of training to fight and to lead. They had all experienced life and death situations and they had all been forced to fight to survive. Now they were collectively powerless – unable to change or improve their situation, unable to plan their future and unable to escape – and all sharing the overwhelming feeling of sheer frustration.

Following her return from the funeral with the suitcase, its contents gradually took up more of her time after work. She sifted carefully through the contents of the old suitcase, trying to put it into an order, and identify the dead-ends where she needed greater knowledge about the Second World War to understand the meaning and significance of the papers. Day by day, week by week, she chose items to follow up on. She sought out maps and publications of all kinds, including official military documents and archives, to back up and fill in the historical gaps.

Little did she know then that the military facts were just the beginning. Her Dadu's personal story that started to emerge from the fascinating contents of the old suitcase would soon account for much more than a few evenings and weekends. As the story grew, it would take over her thoughts, her emotions and every part of her life. She realised that she had to try to step into his time and place to really follow his journey and discover the true message behind this legacy that he had left in her care.

It was her mission and, like her grandfather before her, she was determined to complete it, wherever it may take her next.

In the camp, the days were long and empty, the food poor and the conditions uncomfortable. Through letters they heard that life in many POW camps was much harsher, but that seemed cold comfort.

All of the men were hungry. Their food rations were low – just enough to keep them alive, but not enough to stop them becoming irritable and occasionally emotionally hot-headed. Red Cross food parcels did, however, get through from time to time. These were often designed as packages to be given to individuals to supplement the camp meals, but instead they were collected together by the Italian cooks and placed in the central food store in the kitchens. That meant that the only source of food was the camp kitchen, which was patrolled by the guards, themselves happy to scrounge whatever they could from the cooks.

To get to the food, you had to get to know the guards, so Reg hung around listening. He did not know Italian and it had been playing on his mind ever since the German interrogator had asked him if he knew the language of the country in which he now needed to survive. He sauntered along by the kitchens listening to the guards chatting to each other, trying to pick up a few words. When he wandered past the kitchens for perhaps the sixth time in an hour, one of the guards pointed and said, *'Ancora Lei?'* – You again? Reg laughed and repeated back, *'Ancora!'*

Guessing that this might well mean 'again' or 'more', Reg tried it out as a guard was leaving the kitchen with a handful of items. Before the guard could speak, Reg said, '*Ancora!*' The guard laughed and threw him a stock cube. Reg saved this treat for a quiet moment. Surely the meat extracts would give him some strength! But the wartime 1d. (old penny) cubes were full of salt and it only made him violently sick.

Basic services were, however, supplied and the nuns in the convent next door provided a laundry service to the growing number of officers at the camp. By May 1943 this was 502 Allied servicemen, of which most were army, although 10 were navy and 28 were air force. They were guarded by around 70 Italian soldiers.

Soft power played its part too and, like the Arsenal-loving German officer at the interrogation point, the Italian camp commander was an anglophile. As if to underline the complicated history of Europe and its shifting allegiances, he, Colonel Vicedomini had fought *alongside* the British against Austria in 1917 and remembered the camaraderie of that time with great affection and respect. He liked the company of the British officers and the change in national politics did not alter his personal affinity with the men who now found themselves under his control. His second in command, Captain Mario Jack Camino, had a British mother and wife and had run his own business in Slough before the war. His assistant, Lieutenant Peredini, had been a Thomas Cook representative in peacetime, so knew English too. He would not be arranging any trips for the prisoners just yet, but was at least a customer-facing guard.

Some of the officers knew about Captain Camino's English links, but Reg as yet did not. To John Baddeley and some of the other officers, it seemed like too good an opportunity to miss for a little fun. Besides, the officers were concerned that morale was getting low. The men had activities to distract them from the boredom of confinement, but they also needed to keep presentation standards up if their general hygiene and personal care was not to suffer too. Respect for others also comes from self-respect and if they let themselves become slovenly, discipline might be eroded. However, why not kill two birds with one stone? Why not find a way to boost standards and have a little fun at Selby's expense at the same time? They hatched the perfect plan. They would get Selby to try to arrange for a barber to come to the camp.

With a twinkle in his eye, the most senior officer in their group began, 'Selby, the men are looking very shaggy, don't you think?' He pointed to a few heads. 'Long hair and scruffy collars. You know a few words of the lingo. Why don't you have a go at persuading the guards to bring in a barber? See if you can get that message across to the camp's second in command, Captain Camino over there.'

'But I don't know the Italian for 'haircut' or 'shaving,' replied Selby.

'You'll find a way, old chap!' encouraged his officer friend, John Baddeley, winking and giving him a targeted slap on the back that just happened to steer him in the direction of Camino.

Reg coughed lightly to get the captain's attention, then began gesturing to mime his request. Camino watched, arms folded. He cocked his uniform cap on one side and raised an eyebrow as the gestures continued. Selby mimed lathering his chin with exaggerated gestures, then scraping it off with a finger as the blade, twisting his face and raising his chin to make it realistic.

Camino glanced up at the senior officer and his friends behind Selby, who were struggling to stifle their laughter. John winked at Camino as Selby pretended to take scissors from his pocket with fingers that became scissor blades, pretending to snip hair to the length of a military haircut. By now all the officers and men were holding their sides and weeping with suppressed sniggers.

In the end, Captain Camino, now wiping an eye too, had to end Selby's miming misery. In clear English with barely an Italian lilt, he said, 'Enough! You are an excellent actor, but I can't see you suffer for your art any more. Okay, okay. The barber will come!'

At Selby's open-mouthed reaction to this perfect command of the English language, the wall of restraint behind him collapsed and the men broke out into uncontrolled guffaws.

Shortly after that, the village barber and his lad entered the camp to cut the men's hair, batch by batch. The barber was a serious man, who carried himself with the importance that his respected position in the community as a master of his trade merited. He was short and stocky with a wide face and dark, active eyebrows. He had a balding pate, but bold waves in the remaining dark strands. These seemed to be woven into a kind of cap like a wicker basket over his sun-mottled scalp. He walked heavily, but when cutting hair or shaving with a sharp razor, he was as agile as a dancer. He moved his hands around the heads of the seated soldiers and airmen with the precision of a juggler and with the artistic enjoyment of a flower arranger, even on his hundredth short-back-and-sides. His eyebrows worked as hard as his fingers, moving up and down in line with the demands of each task. As the hours passed, one or other thread from his woven thatch would work loose and bob around his face in time with the sweeping actions of scissors and comb.

The barber's young assistant was about 15 or 16 years old with dark brown hair. It was cut short at the back, but styled with a low side parting in order to grow longer hair across the top of his head. This he allowed to fall forward as a fringed curtain through which to peep and observe the strange world of the camp full of foreigners. Reg thought he spotted a look of admiration in the boy's eyes as the youngster glanced around the room at these international officers. He smiled shyly while watching the men with untidy hair being transformed into crisp, clean, smart officers. He seemed intrigued by the change brought about by a simple haircut and close shave. Men casually leaning against the wall, ungainly and slouching as they queued for a seat, were transformed into officers who stood tall and walked out at a confident semi-march, looking every inch like warriors brave enough to fight the intimidating Nazis.

This assistant swept and tidied, ushering each new solider to the vacant barber's chair, often looking across at the master barber for approval. The barber only needed to say the lad's name, 'Paolo!' and he hurried to do the next task. '*Subito!*' (right away), Paolo replied.

The young apprentice clearly took his work seriously, and sought reassurance and affirmation from his boss. His mouth twitched in a snatched smile each time the barber, acknowledged him with a nod or a flick of one of those wandering, waving strands of hair.

Reg was watching too. He studied them both closely, these local folk from outside the camp. They seemed approachable and when it came to his turn, Reg tried to chat to the boy. He realised that unlike the senior camp officers who had lived in Blighty or learnt languages in earlier wars, this lad would not know English, so he copied the guards' greetings to each other that he had memorised. '*Buongiorno!*' The boy politely replied the same.

Reg tried a few more words.

'English.'

'*Sì, Inglese. Lei, è Inglese.*'

'Ah! In-glay-zay.'

'*Ha, bravo!*'

He pointed to the boy, 'Italian?'

'*Sì. Italiano.*'

'*Ah. Lei è Italiano* – you are Italian.'

'*Sì, bravo!*'

Now that the ice was broken, Reg pressed for more. 'Red Cross?' He made a cross sign with his fingers and pointed to the colour red on a bottle label. The boy was puzzled, then realised what Reg meant. He looked around then winked.

On his next visit, the barber's assistant, Paolo, recognised Reg and, with a swish, put a longer than usual towel around Reg's shoulders. He was about to prepare Reg's hair for the master by combing it through, but then appeared to drop his comb on the floor. He bent down to pick it up and pulled something from his bag, slipping it discreetly under the towel as he stood up.

'*Allora!*' (Okay then), Paolo said brightly, shrugging his shoulders and tugging at his sleeves, the way the master barber did to free his hands for action. He began combing Reg's hair in quick, short strokes, ready for cutting.

Reg was surprised to feel a book on his lap, not a can of food. Slowly and carefully, he slid it under his shirt, pulling his trouser belt tight over the shirt buttons, so it would not slide down when he walked out with his new short-back-and-sides haircut.

Finding a rare quiet corner near the kitchens and waiting patiently until a passing guard had gone by, Reg slid the book out. Turning it over to see the cover, he had to stifle his instant guffaw as he read the title. It was a basic guide to bookkeeping and accountancy – in English! He was not sure how the boy had got it, but assumed it must have been from a Red Cross parcel that had been dropped by parachute since his last haircut conversation. Reg was very grateful, but at first was not sure what to make of this or what to do with it. Perhaps it would relieve the boredom of the daily routine and distract him from the frustrations of hunger on the one hand and the frustrations of feeling unable to help the war effort on the other.

He took it back to his simple bed and slid it under his pillow, thinking no one was around. 'What have you got there, old boy?' came a familiar voice as several men sauntered in. 'Is it spicy? Come on, share!' and a hand lunged forward to snatch the item from under the pillow.

'Bookkeeping and accountancy? Selby, we were hoping for a good look at some juicy *figures*, but that's not what we had in mind!' said the interloper, tossing the book onto the blanket, to the appreciative sniggers of his accompanying crew.

'Well, lads,' countered Reg, thinking fast, 'There are … *countless* opportunities in here – you know this could … *add up* to a brighter future for me – so there's no need to try to … *take away* from my enthusiasm. It may *divide* opinion, but this book could … *multiply* my chances of post-war success!'

'Alright! Alright! Enough of the awful puns! Don't worry, no one's going to be pinching that for a quick peek when you're not looking! Strength to your elbow, Selby. Strength to your elbow!' And with that, he mimed doffing a hat and retreated with the group.

Alone once more, Reg picked up the book and tapped it on his other hand, thoughtfully. 'Future, success… strength… this could be motivational and not just for me.' Instead of putting the book back under the pillow, he strode out to the main activity area, sat as sprawled and relaxed as possible on a randomly placed chair, legs stretched out in front of him, ankles crossed and began reading the book with what appeared to be keen interest and enthusiasm on his face for all to see.

He studied it for a while every day at the same time after that. Around the camp, it got him the nickname, 'The Accountant'. 'Look at him!' joked fellow POW Eric Newby. 'When we leave here *we'll* be eyeing up totty with an hour-glass figure.' '*He'll* be looking at figures to tot up by the hour with an eye-glass!' added another. Reg was glad to hear the banter. It was working! This apparently ridiculous dedication to preparing and planning for what seemed like an impossible, civilian future, was having an effect. It helped them to keep believing in a time with no war, when they would be back home, back to the lives they had left. It seemed to make that dream appear a little closer for them too.

By the time his next haircut came around, Reg was ready with his special word, 'more'. *'Ancora?'* he asked. Paolo was ready too. He had not come empty-handed and was keen to pass on his next delivery to this bold and resolute soldier. This time Paolo had brought a pocket-sized Italian-English dictionary. It was small enough to fit into a jacket pocket but contained enough words to cover most basic conversations.

Reg felt the little book under the towel and could barely contain his excitement to find out what it was. He already had a standard issue *Bible* that was about this size and hoped it was not duplication, but something new, something that could really make a difference in the way that the accountancy book had done. He managed a discrete peep at it under the concealing towel and his heart started to beat faster. This was a real treasure.

Later, in the comparative privacy of the shared dormitory he opened the little book. His fingers trembled a little as he turned the pages. It even had a short grammar section so he could work out how to use the verbs. The Latin roots of the language were familiar and this tiny book opened a significant new path for him. This was a wonderful gift. It opened a route to survival in this foreign land – the possibility of communicating with the ordinary guards, with any outside visitors who came to the camp. It might just give him access to more food or perhaps to other things he might need as the weeks rolled into months and war continued to rage outside.

He immediately set himself targets to learn a certain number of words each day, starting from the letter 'A'. He felt he had already made a start, since he remembered *ancora* (more/again) and *arrivederci* (goodbye). He did not know how to pronounce the words properly, but he sounded out the letters and made the best of it he could – like the Latin of his schooldays.

As the weeks went by, more and more Red Cross parcels were successfully getting through, and a library was set up for the officers to borrow books and spend their time profitably – even if that meant swapping their cigarette rations for more novels. Keeping spirits up became a priority – it helped the men to cope and it helped the guards too, because the men were calmer and had a focus for their days. Reg began to get to grips with bookkeeping systems and little by little his Italian vocabulary crept past the letter 'I'.

The appearance of being busy could also be used as a thinly veiled cover for other activities. As officers, there was an accepted understanding that the detainees had an obligation to try to escape, even if there were no orders to that effect. So, when they got permission to turn some waste land within the camp grounds into a sports area, the prisoners immediately hatched a plan. Within days they had started secretly digging an extra trench down the middle of the new pitch in which to hide men while they waited to escape. The basic plan was that two men would stay outside after sport, and lie in the trench, covered over by teammates so they would remain hidden. After dark, they would creep out and try to escape.

If the plan was to remain secret, the extra soil from the trench had to be taken away somewhere without being noticed. It could not be piled up outside or it would be spotted easily. Then someone came up with the ludicrous but marvellous idea of storing it in the empty loft above their dormitories. This was where Reg found a role. By sitting on the stairs with his books, Reg could keep an inconspicuous look out for guards. The soil was collected and concealed in trouser legs, laundry bags and other everyday containers around the sports area and then men sauntered in from the sports area and up to the roof, past 'The Accountant' on the staircase. Each man deposited a small quantity of soil in the loft space and casually went back outside.

The trench worked, but the escape did not. There were a few other, less sophisticated attempts. Two men even tried to walk out of the camp – dressed as workmen, but perhaps predictably, were soon walked back in. 'What went wrong this time?' Reg asked a returning RAF officer. 'We asked someone for directions. We thought the chap was a helpful peasant, but he turned out to be military in farmer's clothing, out to spot and recapture escapees. We were too naïve, I reckon.'

'Not as naïve as the other pair that left yesterday,' replied Reg.

'Why, what happened to them?'

'They got as far as the railway station on the Parma-Piacenza line, but needed to go to the toilet. Apparently, they went into the ladies instead of the gents – into *SIGNORE* instead of *SIGNORI*! Unfortunately for them, they were reported to the military, who came to get them.'

'Ah.'

'They weren't as lucky as you. They were reportedly taken out and shot.'

'Crikey! I see. So we were very fortunate today to be found by camp guards and taken to our commander. He just gave us a telling off and told us not to do it again! You've got the right idea with your dictionary, you'd have a better chance!'

'And that's all I need,' thought Reg. 'If I get a chance, I'll take it!'

Then, one wondrous day, a special Red Cross parcel arrived. There was great hubbub in the hall and an exceptional roll call sounded. Some letters had got through from home! The men could barely hold ranks as the names were called and the thin folded sheaves, fine as tissue paper were passed around.

He felt his face flush as he heard 'R. Selby?' but just as he was about to step forward to receive a letter from home, he froze, as he saw the guard walk the other way along the line and hand the letter to a New Zealander, Lieutenant Ralf Selby. His ears tingled and flushed red. He swallowed hard. Then 'R. Selby?' was called out again. He must have misheard! John Baddeley, standing next to him, nudged him in the ribs and he sprung forward just in time to take a letter from the pacing guard. He saw at once from the handwriting that his note was from his sister Kathleen.

The men who had received nothing went out to the sports area to kick a ball – just so as to avoid kicking each other in their disappointment. Those with letters dispersed quickly, each looking for a quiet corner in which to spend a moment transported back home. Reg headed for his usual lookout place on the stairs. He took out his accountancy book and laid the letter inside, closing the book over it, as if to keep it safe. He looked up to check he was alone, anticipation making his blue eyes extra bright. Then, slowly, he opened the book, carefully released the seal on the letter and laid it on the pages to read it. He could see Kath sitting at the scrubbed, wooden kitchen table in the Round House Lodge, trying to think what to write, with young Victor making too much noise in the background, and his stepmother busying herself with baking.

Dear Reg,

We have heard so little since the telegram told us you were missing, that we just cling to hope and hard work to get through each day. Father misses you terribly. He says nothing, but I see his heart crack a little more with every silent sunset.

It was wonderful to receive the news that you had been captured! That must sound awful to you, but at least we knew you were alive, even if as a POW.

Father didn't seem to know how to take it, because he was never captured and that was a great matter of pride for him, but secretly, he was relieved too. Of course he never says as much, but he strode off for his Home Guard duties with a slight spring in his step that evening!

Here, the speeches on the radio are very fine, but the news is grim. We have to believe that the tide will turn in our favour soon.

At least at home we have enough to eat. The kitchen garden keeps us well-stocked and there is an abundance of recipes in all the newspapers and magazines telling us how to make the same old vegetables seem a little more exciting.

I hope you are not too hungry – but mainly we hope that you stay alive! Victor declares to all who will listen that, if anyone can find their way home, it's you, Reg. I believe him – and you should too! As the song goes, we'll 'keep the home-fires burning' – to light your way home. I hope you receive this – and with it all our encouragement, hope and love.

Kath.

Reg's bright blue eyes clouded with tears and he blinked them away. He had to hide the moment of happiness. He had to keep home private and safe in order to hold on to the real hope – the hope of getting back to it. He folded the note and was about to enclose it in the book again, when he stopped. He carefully slipped it inside his jacket, and pressed it to his heart instead.

He stared out of the window, across the landscape beyond. England seemed so very far away. What were his chances of getting home? Of being one of the few to survive? He pulled out the letter again slowly and its very touch seemed to warm his hands as if holding it in his fingers showed him he was still alive. 'But I am alive,' he told himself, 'and I wasn't the only survivor in the regiment,' a wry smile crossed his face, 'unlike my father!'

His mind ran back to the day George, the postman, a former soldier like Reg's father, had told him the story about that particular episode in Edward's war.

It was one day when young Reg, aged about nine, was watching for the post. He was expecting a special parcel of a gift he had ordered with his stepmother from the newspaper for his father's birthday. The postman had chuckled at young Reggie's delight on seeing him come up the path, so he had stopped to chat to the lad by the gate. 'It's for my father! Don't tell him though! It's something special!' Reg had blurted out.

The postman put down his postbag and nodded. 'Ah. Well. Your father is a very special man. Do you know why?'

'No. Why? Because he's my dad?'

'Ah young Reggie, that's where you're wrong. He's a very special, very brave soldier.'

'Soldier – yes– I know he *was* a soldier. He's a gardener now!'

'You should know just how special he is. Did you know that he was the only survivor of his whole regiment in the First World War?'

Young Reg had looked confused, staring up at this long-standing friend of his father's. Then he had asked, 'But there is still a regiment, so what happened?'

George, the postman leant on the gate. Reg rarely stood still and seemed to be practising hopping from one foot to the other while George spoke.

'Yes, you're right, lad. There is still a regiment, but with all new members. Because it was only your father who remained from all those brave boys who left here to fight. I joined much later. You know he doesn't talk about the past much, especially not the war. But we former soldiers, we do exchange stories at regimental reunion events sometimes. There are many stories I could tell about your father, but there's one you should definitely know about.'

At this, Reg had stopped hopping. He knew when it was important to listen. He crouched down in his short trousers, placing the parcel by his side, arms around his bare knees to listen and looked up into George's face, curious. 'Tell me, please. I'll listen!'

'Your father joined up right at the start. He was only young himself, but all young men had to go. He worked hard and followed orders to the letter, so he was soon shipped over to France to fight in the trenches.' George paused. 'Terrible it was over there, terrible. But your dad was there for every battle, every attack, brave as you please. Well, you know he got the DSM?'

Reg nodded vigorously. He had seen the shiny medal and its ribbon lying on the dark velvet in its box.

'He was just 23 years old. He was mentioned in despatches and awarded the medal for rescuing a fellow soldier from no-man's-land, that Hell on Earth of mud, barbed wire and death. He got shot in the neck for his efforts, but they both – that is your dad Edward and the wounded soldier – they both made it back to the trenches alive. He saved that man's life and risked his own.' The postman nodded firmly to underline the point, then shook his head, as if shaking off his own memories. Reg looked up at him and tried to imagine the scene he was describing.

Then George continued, 'But then there came a day later on in the war when the Herts men were due to go over the top, out of the trenches towards the enemy at a particularly dangerous place on the front line. It was an especially risky action – they had to try to attack the enemy lines. By then, your dad was the sergeant major, so of course he expected to be with the men, but just before the battle, he was surprised to be called into the officers' dugout.

'Selby, we need you to go back to the quartermaster at the supply post and collect these vital stores for us," says the officer. And he hands your dad a signed order paper. "It's only a few dozen miles, but with all of the chaos it will take time to get there and get back. You must go immediately,' he says.

'But, Sir,' says your dad, 'I need to be with the men for the next attack!'

'Not this, time, Selby. Not this time. That's an order!' he says. 'Now go immediately and be back by sunset tomorrow.'

'Well Edward did not like leaving the men one bit, but an order is an order. He had no choice, did he?'

Reg, without taking his blue eyes off the postman's face, shook his head.

'So, the next day, when Edward returned to the front line with the food rations, he couldn't find the officer to report in. There was no one in their dugout. He thought they must have moved position. That happened a lot, so he asked for directions to the regiment, to deliver the supplies to the right cooks. But do you know what he was told? He was told that his comrades had gone into battle the day before – and that none of them had returned. Not one. They were all dead.' George leant forward with wide eyes to emphasise the point.

Reg's mouth fell open in shock. 'All of them?'

'All. Imagine how that must have felt!' George adjusted his belt as if the very thought of it made him uncomfortable.

Then he went on. 'Your father was sent to report to the senior commanding officer, who told him the news officially. Everyone had been killed on the mission, including the officers. You see, son, it was what they later called a suicide mission. The commanding officers knew that the chances of surviving that attack were close to nil – but they had no choice but to carry out the orders from their superiors. The only 'discretion' as they called it – the only thing they could do – was to choose a soldier who had already served beyond the call of duty and find a reason to remove him from the action. Your father had been through every action since the start of the war. He had served enough, given enough, survived enough. On that day, our Ed was deliberately sent away to the quartermaster's stores on an errand that was not necessary – so that he would not go over the top with the other lads. He was chosen to survive.' George paused. He stood up straight and took a deep breath, looking down at the gate as if it were a gate to past memories that he had opened and had to close again. Then he looked up directly at young Reg. 'And as you can see, he did just that! He's a survivor!' Reg jumped up, grinning, as if to celebrate the good outcome of the tale – at least for his dad.

George the postman paused again, leant forward and ruffled Reggie's light brown hair. 'And that's why you're here now, Reggie, lad!'

Reg the adult, Reg the soldier, Reg the POW, remembered being confused – somewhere between shock, fear and relief – so had just grinned up at the smiling postman who, picking up his postbag had winked and added as he left, 'And I reckon you're a survivor too!'

⁂

The cruellest prison of all is the prison of the mind.
Piri Thomas, *Down these Mean Streets, a Memoir*

Beth took a deep breath. She found she had tears running down her cheeks. After a few silent minutes of staring dully into space, she brushed them away. How brave her great-grandfather was! How brave the officers were who went into battle knowing they would probably die! How utterly incredible that they had the grace, the presence of mind and the generosity to use their limited authority to save a life. Finally, how amazing that her great-grandfather had been such a hero that he was the one man chosen not to die. She propped up the photo of Great-Grandfather Edward wearing his DSM medal against some books beside her computer. Then she placed the photo of her grandfather Dadu beside it. He was also in his uniform and about the same age. Two young soldiers, Edward Selby and Reginald Edward Selby, father and son. Two generations, two world wars, two men in their twenties who gave those 'best years' in combat for their country. She must get them framed – together.

She turned back to the bundle of papers, then looked across to stare at the photos again. Just a minute! What had that story meant to Reg? How did that make him feel? Son of a war hero, son of a man saved from certain death by the deliberate act of his superior officers. How do you live up to that high standard? She felt herself swallow hard. It was then that it really began to dawn on her that he had passed on the responsibility of sharing these valuable stories to *her*! That was her mission! Then she smiled without meaning to – after all, no one was shooting at her, no one was hunting her down, all she had to do was to piece together the separate parts of this lived history. Her generation had got it lucky – so lucky! But then she realised that the pressure was on to make sure that her retelling was worthy of these heroes.

She would make sure she captured each tiny, handwritten message from her Dadu's past. It would not just be a journey of reading, sorting and typing but also of researching. She knew very little about WWII and almost nothing about Italy changing sides in 1943.

At 5.30 last night General Eisenhower, Allied Commander in Chief in the Mediterranean, announced: 'The Italian government has surrendered its armed forces unconditionally. As Allied commander in Chief, I have granted a military armistice, the terms of which have been approved by the governments of the United Kingdom, the United States and the Union of the Soviet Social Republics.'

News Chronicle, London, 9 September 1943

Through the summer, the war raged on outside the camp's walls. Meanwhile, as the front line shifted so did the politics. Suddenly there was a rumour going round that Italy was planning to change sides. As September 1943 rolled into sight, this looked increasingly likely. Within the camp, there was a growing unease – a mixture of hope of imminent release and fear that the camp might be overrun and its POWs sent to Germany. Perhaps instead, they would be caught in the crossfire as the Germans invaded to subdue the Italian forces – their new enemies. It was hard to know how to prepare, so Reg focused on learning as much of the contents of his pocket Italian dictionary as he could. It was a useful distraction, but also a potentially vital skill. The quiet voice in his head repeated the sound advice from his father '…always prepare yourself. The challenges you face may be unknown as yet, but if you have skills, you can find a way through.'

The Allied Governments had anticipated for some months that a change of sides by the Italians might be imminent. Preparations and negotiations began and there was particular concern for the many thousands of POWs in camps in Italy. Winston Churchill had himself been a POW in the Boer War. He had escaped, so he knew only too well the challenges they would face. There was a plan to evacuate as many men as possible once the Allies landed so that, when Italy changed sides, they would not be transferred from Italian hands to German prisons. This plan was only in its early stages of development when intelligence was received that it might already be too late for an evacuation.

Benito Mussolini, the fascist dictator and Prime Minister of Italy for the past 21 years, had already allowed Allied POWs to be transferred to Germany in the final days before his downfall and departure. It became all too clear that the German leadership was keen to make sure the POWs were not released back to the Allies by the Italians when they changed their allegiance from fighting with, to fighting against, Germany. When the Italian Foreign Minister, Raffaele Guariglia refused a request from Germany to send more POWs across the borders into German territory on 20 August 1943, the immediate response was a mass redirection of German troops onto Italian soil. This meant that seven divisions of German troops were in Italy by the end of the month.

Meanwhile, negotiations for Italy to surrender to the Allies were moving forward at a pace. The Instrument of Armistice, through which Italy changed sides in the war to join the Allies, was signed on 3 September 1943 in the Sicilian village of Cassibile, which the Allies had recently recaptured. The news was not made public immediately, because the Allies planned to land troops in Southern Italy with the advantage of surprise. Unfortunately, these landings did not go to plan. Since German forces were already mounting something close to an invasion into Italy from the north, the risks to all those Allied POWs held in Italy were growing with each passing day.

Finally, the public announcement of the Armistice from General Eisenhower came at 6 p.m. on Wednesday, 8 September. It was only reported in London the next day, appearing in the *News Chronicle*.

In Italy, a recorded speech by Marshal Pietro Badoglio, the Italian General who took over as Prime Minister, announced the change of circumstances to the Italian public. It was broadcast from Rome an hour after Eisenhower's announcement. In translation, it ran:

> Italy has been compelled to withdraw from the unequal struggle.... Hostilities by Italian Forces against the Anglo-Americans will now cease on every front. However, our forces will respond to possible attacks from any other quarter.

Badaglio himself was not in the radio station. His government had collapsed and he was preparing to leave Rome with the Royal Family and some fellow Ministers of State in a military convoy. Rome was already surrounded by German forces.

At the camp in Fontanellato, the Italian guards heard the news and, like all Italy, tried to work out what this would mean for them. The announcement was shared with the POWs.

'Do you think they'll send us home?' asked John Baddeley, 'I mean, if the Italians change sides and join the Allies.'

'The Italians might, but I don't think the Nazis will be so generous as to let them do that,' opined one of the other officers. 'We'll be prizes for the Germans to take back home – to their *Heimat* – and use us as negotiating chips in exchange for their own POW officers.'

'As officers, isn't it taken as read that we are supposed to try to escape at every opportunity?' added Reg, 'so if we get the chance, shouldn't we break out?'

'Probably,' added another thoughtfully, 'although there's no back up here and no Allied infrastructure, so we'd be on our own out there.'

'I've heard that there is an Italian resistance – like the French Partisans,' said John Baddeley.

'Sounds like a word I've heard here – *partigiani*,' said Reg thoughtfully. 'We'd have to find them if we're to have a real chance of getting away. England's just too far otherwise.'

'What do you think of waiting for the Allies to get through from the south?' asked John.

Reg had taken any opportunity he could to look at maps on their journey here. He had caught a glimpse of some still posted up on a wall or left open on the front seat of a truck. His months as a navigator while in training back at home had sharpened his orientation abilities. He was still rueful whenever he thought of leading that convoy into the cul-de-sac, but the impact of that day had never left him and neither had the skills he had made sure he developed as a result. He could take in and retain a mass of details from a map with just a few glances. 'I think they'll still be a long way south and the terrain is challenging. I wouldn't count on it.'

'In that case,' added John, 'If you decide to escape, I'm coming with you. I'm blond, burly and don't know a word of Italian. On my own, I'd pass for a native about as well as a giraffe!'

However, nothing was that simple. The official instructions that the camps received were contradictory and many Italian commanders of camps were unsure how or when to act.

⁂ — ⁂

The radio in the Round House Lodge crackled into life. The familiar tones of Prime Minister Winston Churchill reached into the sitting room. 'When he talks, he sounds as if he's eating a very large boiled sweet!' giggled Victor. 'Shshsh!' snapped his father, keen to hear the announcement. Victor duly fell silent. He ducked behind the old armchair. It had horse-hair stuffing coming out in small tufts at the back, where Victor had often picked it when hiding from a scolding. His mother was sitting in it knitting some gloves. She put her work down on her lap to listen more intently. Kath joined them from the kitchen. Tea towel in hand, she stood as ever calm and poised while the announcement played, ready for the news, good or bad, but clearly significant. In the Round House Lodge and in homes all across the land, the familiar voice spoke to them all.

The recorded message was broadcast to let the nation know that Italy had changed allegiance. The country had joined the Allies and was no longer supporting Hitler's forces.

'But what does this mean for Reg, father?' asked Kath, as her father got up to turn the wireless off again.

'You always ask exactly the right question, Kath! What indeed!' He cleared his throat. 'It all depends what the orders are. If they are ordered to stay in the camp, then they will have to wait for the Allies to come and free them. If the Allies are too late, then the Germans will take over the territory and Reg will become a German POW.'

Victor had raised his head above the high back of the chair to listen to his sister and now chimed in, 'What about escape? There have been some escapes reported in the papers, haven't there?'

'Yes, there have,' said his father frowning. 'Officers are expected to try to escape, of course – in fact officers have an unofficial duty to escape! And Reg is an officer.' Edward walked over to the hearth, picked up the fire poker and prodded the glowing logs in the hearth before deciding to share the thoughts on his mind. 'But that's the most dangerous path of all. The chances of getting back alive are slim. Very slim.'

'I suppose this means we won't hear any news from him, or even about him for some time now,' said Victor's mother, patting Victor on the arm as he moved to crouch beside her chair for reassurance.

'No. No news now till…' began the sergeant major, then he cleared his throat again, unable to finish the sentence. He cleared his throat again, returned the poker to the stand, picked up his newspaper and sheltered behind it for the remainder of the evening.

～ — ～

When the announcement that the Italians were changing sides was finally confirmed, the Italian camp commander in Fontanellato did not know what to do. The messages that were coming through were contradictory.

The instruction issued from the Italian War Office on 6 September was that everyone should be released:

> British POWs – prevent them falling into German hands. In the event that it is not possible to defend efficiently all the camps, set at liberty all the white prisoners but keep the blacks in prison.

The instructions from the Allied side on 7 September advised the opposite approach, with a 'stand fast' order to British officers. However, this later turned out to be an old message that had not previously been circulated because it had been part of the evacuation plan that was never finished. Under that plan, the Allies were expecting to re-take the territory and their men:

> In the event of an Allied invasion of Italy, Officers Commanding prison camps will ensure that prisoners of war remain within camp. Authority is granted to all Officers Commanding to take the necessary disciplinary action to prevent individual prisoners of war attempting to re-join their own units.

Commanders in the field who received the message to release the men and the message to keep them in the camps were left to make of it what they could.

Given that there were said to be about 70,000 Commonwealth POWs in Italy at the time, spread across 36 camps and 12 military hospitals, with limited communication channels, the scope for chaos was clear. Within a few weeks of the announcement of the Armistice, it is estimated that around 30,000 Allied POWs were taken from camps by the German forces and 24,000 of them were transported to Germany. That made a total of around 50,000 Allied captives held in Germany by the end of 1943. However, around 30,000 Allied POWs were estimated to still be in Italy. Fewer than 5,000 of those ultimately escaped to Switzerland or elsewhere successfully (4,852 recorded).

The terms of the Armistice agreement with Italy included clauses to ensure the protection of POWs:

> All prisoners or internees of the United Nations are to be immediately turned over to the Allied C-in-C and none of these may now or at any time be evacuated to Germany.

It was expected that the Italians would respect the authority of the Allied Commander-in-Chief. But this did not take into account the actions of the Germans, who were not part of the agreement and who quickly took control of a large part of Italian territory. The forces of the Third Reich would do as they pleased. The well-known phrase from the 1828 US election, coined by Senator William L. Marcy sprang to mind, 'To the victor belong the spoils of the enemy' – and that was not an appealing prospect for the tired and hungry officers in *Campo PG49*. There were rumours that some camps had already turned their POWs over to the arriving Germans and that thousands had been transported from Italy.

The German troops were moving towards Fontenellato faster than expected and it made the Italian camp commander uneasy. He consulted his deputy and camp leaders of the POWs of different nationalities. Lieutenant Colonel Hugo de Burgh, Senior British Officer at the camp was particularly keen not to wait to be captured by the Nazi forces, which he felt was likely. *Colonello* Vicedomini agreed that they needed a plan. He told the guards that their job was to protect the prisoners of war, though he doubted how long they could hold the camp in the face of a German attack if sufficient well-equipped enemy forces swooped in.

Long discussions led to a compromise decision. They collectively agreed that they would follow both instructions as a two-part approach! They would all stay in the camp until they heard that the Germans – now the enemy – were close, then they would all leave – the POWs and the Italian guards.

The POWs were called to the parade ground to hear the decision. The situation was explained and the instructions given. They would all eat dinner that evening and pack their belongs before lights out, ready to depart. The next day, the men were to wear battle dress. They would be given a day's rations and some Italian Lire. A morning snack would be distributed and they would have salmon and boiled potatoes for lunch, prepared by Lieutenant Blanchaert and the kitchen team.

When the time was right, a bugler would sound the signal, three 'G' notes, and *Capitano* Camino would march the POWs out of the camp in a column to a sheltered local valley, about five miles to the north-west in the gorge of the Rovacchia Stream and wait there for further developments.

After the briefing, the POWs discussed the plan amongst themselves. Many felt that being led in such a large marching group to a known gully nearby made them sitting ducks. While most POWs decided to stay, some decided to make a break for it. These expected that the commander would turn a blind eye if anyone walked out of the camp and made their own way.

Camp guards were posted as lookouts by the commander to signal if German Third Reich forces were getting close.

It was not long before the alarm sounded. The new enemy had swooped in fast from the north to secure the territory before the Allies could advance from the south. They had already been sighted just two miles from the camp. Lunch was off. In short order, all the prisoners were marched out. The remaining guards stood at their posts for a while, but swiftly melted away in civilian dress back to their village homes.

The local peasants knew all about what was happening and wanted to support the escaping POWs who went to the valley. With their knowledge of the landscape, these generous farming folk easily found the prisoners. The locals provided them with food parcels, which was very kind, but it also showed the prisoners that the Germans were not going to take long to trace them. It was agreed that they should all split up and set off to find their own way – it was every man for himself.

Not all the POWs still had full battle dress. They were wearing a mixture of military clothes and civilian garments that had been supplied by the Red Cross over the months of imprisonment. This meant they were vulnerable to being shot if found by German soldiers. It was hard to decide how to present themselves. Full uniform should protect them from being shot, but would make them very obvious as escapees. Full or part civilian dress gave them no protection under the rules of war. Many still had their military boots, which was a great giveaway to anyone looking for POWs, but the men were very reluctant to leave them behind as they knew they had a hard road ahead and the boots still represented the best footwear around.

Moreover, with so many men all trying to escape and find shelter at the same time, there would be competition for local help. In these hard times, there would also be a strong incentive for unscrupulous or desperate locals to hand men over to the enemy for a reward. It was a very real threat and the risk for the POWs was that offers of help would evaporate, as soon as the first few escapees were found and the first civilians were shot for collaborating. The Third Reich made no bones about the savage, uncompromising reprisals that would be meted out for collaborating with the enemy. German propaganda made clear that if they found collaborators, the POW and the host families, including the children, would be punished with summary execution. Furthermore, their houses would be raided for food and anything valuable. Then the house or farm would be burnt down.

Before the men could worry about who would help them, the question they needed to answer was, 'which way to go?' About two-thirds headed south to try to meet up with the Allies, who had landed at Salerno and captured Naples. However, progress for these escapees would be limited by the German defensive lines across the country, the Bernhardt and Gustav Lines. There was also a well-defended German position to get past in the Abbey on the high rocky hill at Monte Cassino, a superb natural fortress. The Italians shook their heads at any suggestion of attempting this route. They knew it was completely impractical.

But escape was not a choice – it was, despite all the hazards, a simple necessity. Those who broke away early generally went in pairs, in line with recommended practice.

'Are you going now, Reg?' asked Captain John Baddeley of the Hampshire Regiment.

'I'm thinking of doing so,' replied Reg, scanning the view outside the camp.

'Then let's go together!'

'Thanks, John. It would be an honour and a pleasure! I've been looking at the landscape. To me, the route to the Allies goes through too much enemy-held land, so I'm going to bet on joining the partisans in this area. They must have access to food and weapons, so while communism may not be my bag, at least we'll be on the same side.'

'Sound thinking, Selby. I'm with you!'

Reg and John set out to the south-west and headed for the higher ground that they could see on the horizon. From rumours in the camp, they believed the Communist partisans, who were still fighting the Italian Army, were based there.

Within hours, the rumble of tanks on the roads could be heard as Nazi reinforcements started searching the surrounding area, drawing ever closer to Fontanellato. Then a fleet of *Kübelwagen* (Nazi jeeps) swept into the main square and armed men quickly overran the camp.

The German commanding officer had the camp commander brought before him. He demanded to know where the prisoners were. But before the Italian could even reply, he was struck in the face and fell to the ground. It was a rhetorical question. This brave man was arrested for letting the POWs go. He was summarily despatched as a traitor to a concentration camp in Poland. Any other remaining Italian guards became POWs themselves and the gates were once again firmly locked.

The salmon and boiled potatoes that stood ready in the kitchen was immediately commandeered by the new military occupants. One of the Germans found the key to the wine store. The allies-turned-enemies caroused late into the night.

Out in the surrounding countryside, the escaping POWs had left with almost nothing – a minimum of rations, no spare clothing, no bedding and of course no weapons. It was a question of survive or die. They reckoned that the Germans would focus their initial search around the camp, so the further away they could get at speed, the greater their chances of slipping through the tightening net of enemy forces.

Using the landscape and the sun for orientation, Reg and John headed towards the hilly area near Salsomaggiore, south of Fidenza and for the next two days, they ran for as much of the day and night as they dared, stopping to hide in vineyards to rest or eat the unripe grapes for food and liquid. The bitter skins and still unripe flesh of the fruit churned in their weak stomachs, but there was nothing else, so they struggled on. Once, they stopped to sleep in the dark on a ledge under a bridge, only to be woken by the rumble of an entire column of Nazi military vehicles passing across above them. It was just too risky to stay still.

On the afternoon of the third day, as they were crossing a field of cut hay dotted with haystacks, a *Kübelwagen* appeared on the nearby road from round the bend with four soldiers inside. 'In there!' whispered Reg.

They each dived into a different haystack. Reg crouched very still, heart pounding, cocooned in his mess of cut crop, listening, listening. Suddenly everything seemed so vivid. He could smell the hay and feel the warm energy from its fermenting mass around him. As his eyes adjusted to the dark, the many shades of gold from white to almost brown gleamed matt and clear in the tiny chinks and splinters of light that filtered through. He dared not move a muscle in case it made a rustling sound or caused a shake visible from the outside, although his

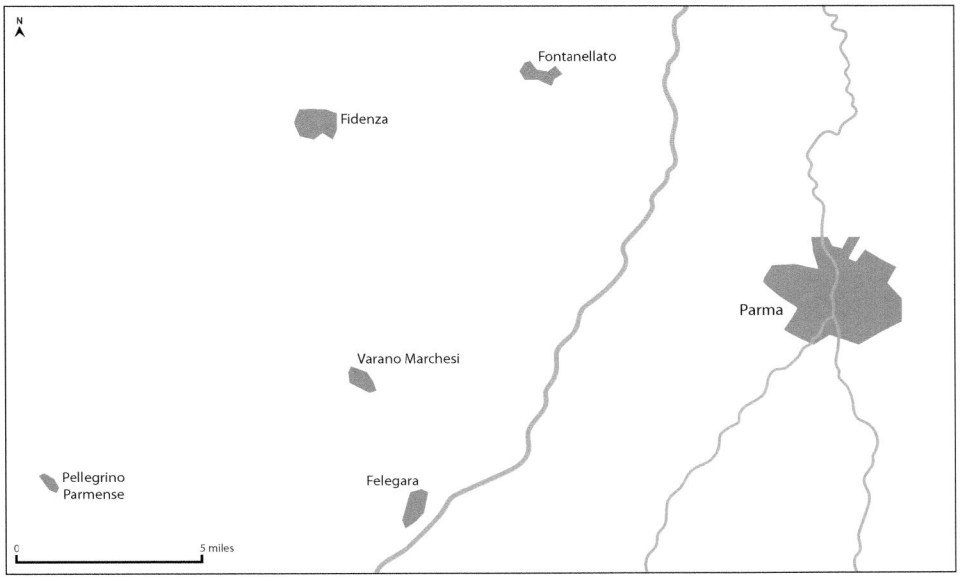

Map showing the key locations of Parma, Fontanellato, Pellegrino Parmense and
Varano Marchesi.

limbs soon started to stiffen. The sharply cut ends of the stalks held him lightly
but firmly in place, like so many pins holding a living butterfly.

He heard the *Kübelwagen* engine stop, and voices as the men got out to search.
They called to each other in German from different directions as they fanned out,
scouring the ground. They were hunting for escapees. The sounds of bayonets
slicing through straw, as they speared the haystacks, were as sharp and close as if
next to his ears. Perhaps this was standard procedure, or perhaps they had spotted
a movement.

His own breathing and the beating of his heart seemed as loud as a piston
straining to set an engine in motion and set off down the rails. Would they hear
him? Would they spot his tracks? At least there was no barking. If they had dogs,
it was all over. They would be sniffed out and snuffed out in seconds. No dogs.
There was still hope that they would pass him by.

Suddenly a piercing scream rang out, long and terrifying. It hung in the air.
Reg shivered from head to foot then fought to control his shaking body as the
sound of more blades slashing into a haystack brought screams, then moans, then
silence. The shocking thought ran through his brain like melting ice. John. They
must have found John! Rage for this merciless slaughter of his friend wrestled in
his chest with deep fear for himself, the two emotions writhing as they battled for

dominance. He wanted to burst out of his straw cocoon and fight the aggressors with his bare hands yet he wanted to vanish like a butterfly perfectly camouflaged by closing its wings on a matching leaf. Fear held his anger still, and anger stilled his shivering fear. He hung in place, suspended as the seconds stretched on around him.

He listened with an intensity he had learnt in this war. Listening as never before with that ever vigilant sense that might now just save his life. To his surprise, the sound of the voices became softer and appeared to be retreating back to their vehicles. Were they talking instead of shouting? No longer loud, urgent calls of instructions. The phrases were longer, less clipped and calmer. It was conversation, relaxed, then at last what sounded like a decision, an order to leave. The *Kübelwagen* engine started again, its rumble soon fading as it drove away till it was barely audible behind the natural veil of buzzing summer insects and snatches of bird song.

Reg's shoulders began to relax and he prepared to move. 'But wait, wait!' his inner voice shouted. He remembered how the Nazis played tricks to flush POWs out, making it seem that they had gone, but leaving two soldiers behind to shoot whatever emerged timidly into the new silence, gunning them down where they stood. No. No, they would not catch him like that! He breathed deliberately, evenly, slowly and composed himself, ready to listen again.

It was getting dark when Reg finally dared to crawl out and look around. Grey shadows were stretching lengthening fingers across to reclaim the golden field. Everything was quiet. There was no sign of John. The haystack Reg thought John had chosen to hide in was broken open, but there was nobody here. Neither were there any traces of blood. Had they taken him? Had they killed him silently, a hand over his mouth? If so, who had screamed? He furrowed his brow, confused, but determined to find out what had just happened.

Across to the right, he saw another broken stack. He trotted lightly over to it, still alert and looking around as he did. There, sprawled across the tangled straw, lay a bloodied body, limbs oddly angled like the bent and scattered golden blades. Dark patches settled around his many gashes – a vision of a 'Saint Sebastian of the bayonets' in the gloom. Reg swallowed hard and leant in closer, perhaps to close the eyes forever of his friend and companion.

It was not John! The Nazis had found a different victim; one he did not recognise. His hand shook and he hesitated, taken aback at seeing the stranger's face. A stranger, but a fellow escapee, no doubt. A young man with a family and home, somewhere. He gently stretched out his hand and closed the staring eyes with trembling fingers before straightening up to look at this soldier, this man, like him. His instinct was to say a prayer. The sounds and rhythms from so many church services back in Ware began running automatically through his head. His dry lips shaped the silent verses gently, as he looked down at this man, then up to the darkening sky, tears slowly trickling from his eyes.

After a silence that seemed to last too long, Reg suddenly became aware of being alone. Alone in the field. Alone in this land. Alone in the war. He should bury his countryman, he thought, but no. That would take time and put his own life even more at risk. He had to leave this fellow to the kindness and humanity of the farmer who owned the land to give him some last rites. Reg had to save himself and go on alone.

Looking around to check the perimeter of the field for any signs that the attackers were returning, he made for the cover of the hedge and skirted the field in its lengthening shadow. Just as he turned onto the road, fingers grabbed his sleeve and pulled him behind the roadside trees, covering his mouth with a hand. He was about to struggle. 'Reg!' a familiar voice whispered urgently in his ear. 'It's me, John!' They hugged and silently laughed with joy to see each other alive, then both instinctively looked back at the field to where their unknown comrade lay. With a nod of understanding, but without a word, the two men turned slowly, respectfully and soundlessly saluted. Then John pointed up the road, Reg nodded and they set off as fast as they dared.

5

I Partigiani, The Partisan Fighters

The only way to deal with an unfree world is to become so absolutely
free that your very existence is an act of rebellion.
Albert Camus, *the Myth of Sisyphus*

By the fourth morning, they were in the foothills, but their strength was failing.
Autumn nights in the damp fields and too many meals of immature grapes had
weakened stomach and resistance. Around mid-afternoon, they stopped to rest
in a vineyard with farm buildings nearby and sheltered in the shade of the hedge.
John lay down and closed his eyes. Reg sat and lifted his face to the glow of the
September sun. Its warmth blessed his head and wrapped him in a welcome, if
fleeting, feeling of familiarity and security. He sighed and took a deep breath of
perfumed air. He smelled the dry soil and wild herbs, saw the light fall through
the vine leaves dappling the vineyard with dancing shadows in the fickle, warm
breeze. Closing his eyes, the gentle sounds of the bees and distant birdsong wafted
in and out of his sightless consciousness. He felt himself moulding into the landscape, drifting away into the release of sleep.

Crack! The sound of a boot on a stick startled his every nerve back to the
present moment. John stirred and Reg grabbed John's shoulder to hold him still,
as his own tired eyes darted around the field, squinting in the sudden brightness.

Meandering into the vineyard came a boy of about 12 years old, wearing a rough
working shirt, trousers to his knees, long socks and sturdy boots – boots that had
cracked the twig. He walked unwillingly, lazily swinging a wicker basket. He
strolled along the rows of vines, checking the stems and leaves for signs of insect
infestation or blight, picking a leaf or grape now and then to put in the basket and
take back as evidence that the task was done.

Reg watched the relaxed and regular movements of the boy. He seemed calm,
not the type to react hysterically, scream or shout. 'I have to take a chance,' Reg

thought. He pulled together some of the words he had learnt, nodded at John to stay put and stepped out of the slanting shadows.

The boy stumbled back at the sight of the dishevelled, dusty man. '*Partigiani?*' said Reg hopefully with a terribly un-Italian accent. The boy looked confused, but Reg did not want him to run away, so he pressed on, '*Inglese, soldato, aiuto, per favore!*' (English, soldier, help, please)

The boy relaxed and grinned. '*Inglese!*' he said. Then his expression changed to serious, and alert too. He signalled to Reg to duck down. Reg beckoned and John scrambled to join them while Reg again reassured the boy, '*Due Inglesi!*' (Two Englishmen), he whispered, and the lad nodded.

With one hand on Reg's shoulder to keep him stooped below the tops of the vines as they ran, the boy led the starving soldiers through a maze of vineyards. Then they ran, crouching all the way, down past rough dry-stone walls and through small hillside fields. Finally, they reached the main yard with its barns and outbuildings, and then, hot, fearful and hungry, they were ushered through an old doorway. They passed under crooked wooden beams, and saw that the boy had brought them to the cool shelter of the farmhouse kitchen.

'*Papà! Inglesi!*' the boy called to his father, who was poring over a tall, narrow black book of what looked like scribbled accounts on the large wooden kitchen table. The father stood up, looking serious and determined. He swiftly cast an eye over the scrawny men, then smiled broadly and clapped a strong hand on Reg's back. '*Benvenuto!*' (Welcome!)

Reg had struck lucky. This family was on the side of the partisans and would not give them up to the Nazis. The boy fetched a jug of clean water and two chunks of freshly baked bread, earning him a welcome grunt of approval from his father. Reg felt the clean water trickle down the inside of his parched throat – more valuable than liquid silver – and took a small bite of the bread, afraid to choke if he bit too much at once. Grateful tears welled up in his eyes as the taste of home, even a foreign home, touched his tongue.

These weary men were given soap and water to wash and a place to rest while they waited for nightfall. That evening, after dark, the vine grower and his boy led Reg and John, refreshed, though still in their dirty clothes, up old overgrown footpaths to the small hillside village of Pellegrino Parmense. They climbed for some time, finally reaching a lane lined with cottages. Although by all accounts there should be no German soldiers here, the boy held Reg back as they left the cover of hedges thick with wild roses, and reached the edge of the rough country road. He put a finger across his lips, silently shaking his head. The curfew meant that only those enforcing the rules should be out at this time, so any sound would be suspicious. The next steps must be taken with caution.

The boy listened for footsteps for a moment, then slowly moved forward to glance along the lane in each direction, before signalling for his father, John and Reg to follow. They slipped past two houses and then tiptoed through the yard of the third and round to the back door. A young man in a dark, boiled wool working jacket was leaning against the door, slowly smoking a cigarette. The boy made an owl call and the man stood upright, placing his hand quickly to his side, presumably where he had a weapon ready. The boy walked out of the shadows and the two youthful partisans nodded to each other. The *Inglesi* and the vintner stole across the yard and in through the opened back door.

Inside, a man in his thirties with dark hair and glasses was crouched in front of a small wood-fired stove, poking it to stoke it brighter. He stood up and acknowledged the vintner and his son and then greeted the two foreign refugees, '*Buona sera*' (Good evening), and indicated the empty chairs and kitchen stool.

He offered to share the meal he was about to cook, but which itself was slowly trying to escape that fate. Garden snails were placed on a baking tray, still alive. The guests declined, so he shrugged and pushed the tray into the hot, wood-fired oven. While the creatures squealed, he turned and sat back at the table to examine his guests more closely.

The head of the partisans was no burly brigand. His calm and thoughtful face, with clear brown eyes and soft, clean-shaven cheeks had the appearance of a self-educated leader, keen to use his knowledge to improve society. As Reg was to discover in later conversations, the path he had chosen was Communism against Fascism and he was living at a time when men with these qualities were needed in every parish. He had taken on the role of leader in the area around Fontanellato for ideological reasons. He dismissed the young watchman with an appreciative flick of his head and, with a nod, he resumed his post near the door. The leader then turned his attention fully to the new arrivals.

Carefully setting aside the crumpled map of the hills that he had been studying by the low flame of a gas lamp, the leader looked to the boy for a fuller explanation.

The vintner's lad happily explained. '*Ho trovato gli Inglesi nel vigneto,*' (I found the Englishmen in the vineyard) he explained. The smart partisan lifted his dark eyes and shot a sparkling glance at the escapees. His intellectual face broke into a generous smile. '*Bravo, Marco*' (Well done). Then he turned to Lieutenant Selby and spoke in clear Italian, 'So you were in our village vineyards – you like our wine, *Inglese*?' he asked with a wink at the vintner and a smile. Selby understood a little of this and repeated 'wine, *vino*', returning the brigand leader's smile with his own. Marco's father nodded. He lifted the flagon of wine he had been carrying and put it on the table. The look-out brought two handfuls of small glass tumblers and the vintner poured. They drank with a toast to freedom. The first taste of the rich, intoxicating ruby liquid filled Reg's senses with a glorious exhilaration. The flavours swirled around his tongue and a burst of heat flooded his head.

To Selby's surprise, the leader then asked the look-out to fetch the other Englishmen, *'Gli altri Inglesi.'*

'Other Englishmen?' repeated Reg and he and John exchanged surprised and expectant glances. Who else had found this place? They must be from the camp too!

A moment later, two other officers from the camp stepped into the room. The relief of the men to see each other alive and in safe hands released itself in hugs followed by more toasts with the delicious, deep red wine. The vintner joked that Pellegrino was as busy with Englishmen as the famous Piccadilly Circus these days and gave Reg another friendly slap on the back.

Some men have a natural authority through their presence alone. The head of the partisans gave a simple wave and everyone knew that the greetings were over. It was time to focus and get to the business in hand. He calmly and clearly explained that brave but poor families, tenant farmers in the hillside villages had volunteered to shelter Allied servicemen who had escaped or been shot down. The little they had, they would share.

Gently pushing his spectacles back up the bridge of his nose, he quietly outlined the risk that these people were taking. If the English were discovered in the community by German forces, they would be shot on sight. Out of uniform they were not protected as prisoners of war. Reg translated as best he could, checking his understanding with gestures, where necessary. 'See,' he commented as an aside to his newly rediscovered comrades, 'that miming practice in the camp has come in handy after all!'

This was no time for joking however and the leader's flat facial expression reasserted the seriousness of his message. He waited for silence and quietly continued, 'You may be shot. You may lose your lives here. However, your host families, the farmers, have more to lose. Their houses will be burnt down, their livestock taken. They will almost certainly sacrifice their own lives and,' he let this reality sink in and then added softly, 'their children will be shot too.'

There was no mercy in this war and everyone was a fighter, however young. The families were not in uniform, not on the front line, but they too were risking everything for the idea of freedom.

He waited a few moments for the implications of that message to be fully understood, then the leader of the partisans continued. 'In return for this support, I have a request for our cause. You are trained and experienced fighters, so you will be asked to assist the partisans whenever you are called upon to join our activities. We shall run raids from time to time and your skills will be valuable to us.'

Reg did his best to translate, and finally the English soldiers nodded solemnly and they all shook hands. The leader added. 'Perhaps you have not heard, but the camp commandant stayed behind when the prisoners left. Within just two hours, a troop of around 30 Germans arrived. When *Colonnello* Vicedomini showed them the paper that he had received instructing him to release the prisoners, the Nazi commander struck him to the floor and gave the order to take him prisoner in your place and send him to a camp.' He paused, and Reg asked questions to check that he had understood correctly before sharing this upsetting news with the escapees. The quiet Communist freedom-fighter watched them as they slowly took this in. His dark eyes glinted behind his spectacles as he looked from man to man, checking to see if they would really care what happened to his countryman, their considerate camp commander. The response was instant – clear anger, frustration and sadness. Now the partisan turned his focus to the escapees. This was clearly not his first reception and induction of enemy forces that needed to be hidden. He had a prepared process and agenda. It was important that the Allied men understood their own position too. The war was not over for them. The next chapter had only just begun and it brought with it new risks, new challenges and new responsibilities.

'We expect the authorities to put a price on your heads, so there will be a reward if anyone who sees you decides to hand you in. You must take no risks with your own or your hosts' lives. Do you understand? Now, do you still accept our protection?'

The English soldiers exchanged solemn looks and then each nodded agreement.

'Good. Then you will be billeted with friendly families in Pellegrino Parmense or Varano Marchesi, depending on where we can find room. You will be moved as and when we feel it is necessary for the safety of the host families and for your own protection.' Again he paused.

'However, you must hide well and do just as the families say. Remember, more than your own lives depend on it.'

The snails had stopped squealing, so were deemed cooked. The partisan left the table to fetch his dinner and the soldiers and locals took up the conversation. With some patchy translation, gestures and jabbing at the crinkled map, the young partisan who had remained standing by the door, stepped forward and explained, 'The Germans win at the lower levels every time. They have superior firearms and more men. But we make sure they struggle to beat us above 600 metres. Up here in the hills, the partisan sniper rules the roost!' He clapped his hand on the rifle at his side and laughed. Looking at the still solemn faces around the table, he poured more wine and encouraged everyone to drink up. 'With your help, we shall push them further downhill like children on sledges in the snow. Whoosh!' He added, raising one arm in the air and swooping it onto the table, from which he grabbed his glass, raised it to his mouth and sent the red wine swirling down his throat.

6

On the Trail in Emilia-Romagna

If we could read the secret history of our enemies, we should find in each man's life, sorrow and suffering enough to disarm all hostility.

Henry Wadsworth Longfellow,
Driftwood: A collection of Essays, 'Table Talk', 1857, p.452

When Beth first read the notes about this episode, it had been on that very first occasion, the day after she had returned home to her London flat after her grandfather's funeral. Reading it again, Beth thought about how young her grandfather had been at that time. She was now about the same age as he had been when he experienced such fear and constant threat. No wonder wartime had left an impression that the years could not soften. And yet, his memories of Italy seemed to be good. Why would he still love the music and feel close to it? This must be just the start of her grandfather's story.

After her late night looking through the first batches of notes and then a long series of evenings of reading and note taking, she had suddenly felt incredibly tired. The funeral already seemed so long ago. Her whole life had shifted in the time since then. It was not that her current reality had changed. Her flat was the same, her room, her work. In that sense, her present was just as before – but the past? The past had altered completely.

It felt as if black and white images flickering in old films and newsreels from a long ago, distant time had cast their living light unbidden onto her modern reality. As she picked up the bundles of other documents spread out in front of her, to place them back in the case for tonight, she realised that she was holding pieces of the past in her hands. She had opened a small brown leather suitcase and released the genie of her grandfather's history. It now held her spellbound and with only one wish – to find out more.

But right now, she had to sleep. She needed to pace herself and try to plan, to set a framework that would be manageable alongside her job and other commitments. She decided to take some time off work as soon as possible to go to London's Imperial War Museum and to see the army records in the National Archives at Kew. They were supposed to keep all the wartime reports and she hoped that would be the place to start to fill in the background to this personal story.

The sky above London was streaked with the last rays of light. The day had passed in a blur. Exhausted, her legs stiff from sitting and her head spinning with thoughts, she stretched slowly and got up. She put the suitcase and contents carefully on the kitchen worksurface, closed her computer and flopped gratefully into bed to sleep.

Later that week, Beth set off for the Imperial War Museum to start the first stage of her own independent research. She was excited, but also nervous. She booked a time in the silent Reading Room and spent her day searching through endless files and catalogues, but she could find no trace of what she was looking for. She asked the librarians and showed them her notes. They too drew a blank. No reports, no records.

Disappointed, she was just packing her meagre notes back into her folder, when the calling card from the young solicitor Robert Palmer fell out from between the pages. She picked it up, sighed, and then shrugged. 'Worth a try,' she thought. 'Perhaps his father can help.'

Full of frustration at not being able to find any more records, she stood outside the museum building on the windy green lawn and rang the number. 'Hello, is Robert Palmer there, please?'

'Er, yes, he is,' came the reply in his distinctive speaking tone. Then, as if he had just remembered, he added, 'Actually, it's Robert speaking. Can I help you?'

Beth explained. 'Hello Mr Palmer – Robert. I am Beth Selby. Do you remember? You gave me my grandfather's old suitcase and a letter at his funeral.'

'Hello! Yes of course I remember. How can I help you?'

'Thank you. I'm hoping you can. I was wondering if you have any more ideas as to where I might find more information about his time in the army. I've drawn a blank in the war records office, but feel sure there must be more documents somewhere. A researcher in the Reading Room at the Imperial War Museum told me that all escaping officers had to be debriefed on arrival in Switzerland and that the reports made by officers were always kept.'

'I see. So where was he debriefed?' Robert asked.

'Oh! That's a good question, I admit I'd assumed it had happened in the UK, but perhaps not. Perhaps the report was filed in Italy, or in Switzerland...' She felt slightly foolish that she had called him so quickly, without thinking more about her question. She had not yet even checked everything in the suitcase, so she thanked Robert, rang off, and went home.

Back in her flat she decided to prepare better this time. She set up her laptop to one side of her, a glass of water to hand and the old brown suitcase in the centre in front of her. She sat down cross-legged, opened the lid and fondly smoothed the letter from Dadu in its envelope.

Setting the notes about the North Africa campaign carefully to one side, she took out the next layer of documents. These were some large, folded maps of East Anglia that seemed to have been printed on something like thick wallpaper. They were slightly waxy and the paper looked woven. Perhaps these were special wartime travel maps that were sturdier than the later paper versions. Then she remembered – it must have been very hard to get maps at all then. If even the road signs had been taken down, surely you could not simply go into a shop and buy a map. No wonder he had kept these. They must have been the wartime equivalent of treasure!

Under the maps, she noticed a small package in one corner of the suitcase. It was wrapped in brown paper and tied with the red document tape. Undoing it carefully, she found inside a small Bible and a tiny, brown, pocket English-Italian dictionary. 'The dictionary! Here it is! After all these years!' she could not help exclaiming out loud though there was no one to hear or to share her delight. Not only were these such personal and significant possessions, they were also more evidence for her research!

Then she turned to the *Bible*. She carefully lifted the front cover, afraid this sudden activity after so many years might crack the spine. It was, as Beth soon saw, a standard issue army *Bible*. Yes, it had his name written inside. Putting it down gently, she turned to the little dictionary. She picked up the fragile book carefully with both hands. Strangely, the cover and the pages were warped and crinkled, as if they had at some time been wet. None of the maps looked like that, so how had this happened?

A sudden sound made her jump. It was her phone ringing. She got up stiffly and stretched across to grab her mobile. It was Robert ringing back. 'Hi, Beth. I've asked my dad and he says that he does not know any more about it. Everything he had is in the suitcase, so perhaps go to Italy and ask?'

'Italy! Go to Italy? Ask who?' thought Beth, a little irritated, but then a rush of excitement hit her. She realised that she did actually want to go to Italy. Yes – she wanted to see Fontanellato, the village with the castle in the middle, and follow whichever of these notes or documents took her to the next step. So instead, she replied calmly, 'Good idea. I'll go.' Then before she could stop herself, she blurted out, 'Would you like to come? Perhaps you can help.' She was not quite sure why she had asked him. Perhaps because he had already shown that his quirky way of asking an obvious question was actually helpful. Or perhaps because she found him funny and that also might be a handy asset on this possibly dark journey.

There was a second's silence at the other end of the phone, then a sound that perhaps a crab might make if it cleared its throat. 'I reckon my dad can do without me for a few days,' he said, then, as if he couldn't stop excusing himself, once he had started, added, 'To be frank, I think he'd be grateful. I managed to scan in a 140-page document with alternate pages upside down this morning and his client was not impressed. I made some joke about my father's firm doing everything possible for clients, even standing on our heads, which made him laugh, but my dad was not amused. I had to do it again quickly and apologise a lot. So yeah, I'll take a few days' leave and join you.'

Beth and her new solicitor friend, Robert, landed at the Giuseppe Verdi airport, just outside Parma on a hot, dry summer's day. The colours here in Emilia-Romagna seemed intense and bright and there were summer flowers everywhere. From the airport, it was a taxi ride to Fontanellato. Beth had read about the village, with its grand old moated castle and the former POW camp. She had found that the camp was part of three buildings on the Viale Novembre. This matched her research which had said that they were built originally by the Dominican Order of Preachers. One was the Sanctuary, the next was a Monastery and the third was to have been an orphanage until it was commandeered for prisoners of war.

It was not long before Beth and Robert had settled into their respective rooms at a small hotel. Beth was keen to start their search that very afternoon and, after the airless plane and airport, a walk would in any case be welcome. They headed for the main attraction – the Castle of Sanvitale and walked around it, admiring its striking position. After the journey it was good to feel relaxed and it felt rather like a holiday. The castle was surrounded by a paved piazza-like ring of buildings with shops and cafés. It had a welcoming, tourist-friendly atmosphere. Some older gentlemen, perhaps in their seventies or eighties, were sitting around a table on the street outside one of the cafés on a more shaded side of the castle, chatting and passing the time of day. Beth and Robert decided to go over to ask them for directions to the former POW camp. They had to start somewhere and although the war was a long time ago, it seemed likely that it would have been a well-known building in the community.

The group of sun-crinkled faces, some jolly, some glum, all brightened as the young woman with bouncy, curling auburn hair walked directly towards them. Beth had prepared a few phrases on the plane and, consulting the old Italian dictionary asked in halting Italian, *'Dov'è il Campo di Concentramento per favore?'* (Where is the concentration camp, please?)

The men looked up in blank-faced shock for a moment. That is not what they were expecting at all. Then they looked at each other and burst out laughing! They laughed so long that they cried and several had to hold on to each other to avoid accidentally tipping themselves off their chairs. Beth and Robert looked on bemused The bartender came out with his large white apron pinned around his wide midriff and waved at the elderly crew. 'What's the joke, you old goats?' he taunted, 'What are you bleating and laughing about now?' When the first one recovered enough to speak, he said, 'The young lady is asking for the concentration camp!' Then, another, catching his breath, added, *'Dov'è il barbiere? Abbiamo bisogno del barbiere!'* (Where is the barber? We need the barber!) – a comment that set the rest of the crew chuckling again.

The barman shook his head, led Beth and Robert to a table and said in broken English, 'You wait. I bring coffee and get the barber. The concentration camp was a school after war. I go school there. Now is hospital, so is funny to us to hear you say "*campo*". No worry. Is funny to these old men too, as you see!' he said, tutting and gesturing to the recovering men. They were still wiping the tears of laughter from the folds of their faces.

Beth did not want to seem rude, so waited till the barman had gone before checking the dictionary on her phone. Whispering to Robert, 'Very odd. I *think* he said we need the barber. Why do we need a barber?'

Robert shrugged. 'I don't know,' adding with a wry smile, 'perhaps it's a code word round here for the police, or the *mafia*. One of the two.'

Beth did not find this particularly helpful. It was in fact slightly worrying – but if a lawyer was not concerned – even a bad lawyer, then perhaps she should just wait and see.

Then Beth started in her seat. It suddenly dawned on her who this old man must be! Could it be, could it really be? Had they actually found *the* barber's young assistant from the camp? After all these years? It was still just possible.

The coffee arrived quickly, but the barber took a little longer. Eventually, after what seemed like several minutes, a man appeared from the corner of the square. It was hard to tell his age but he had one foot in plaster. He was walking with a stick, progressing in jolting, rocking, stiff strides like a three-legged stool moving forward one stump at a time. As soon as they saw him, the group of his old pals started a croaky banter across the square. Their exchanges and pauses for echoing cackles lasted the full hundred remaining yards of his slow walk. Punctuating his journey with the waving of the stick to add emphasis to his words, the barber eventually arrived with a puff, a pant and a bow. 'He fell off his *bicicletta*, his bicycle,' the waiter explained to Beth and Robert, 'Broke his foot. These old fools joke about his stick. They say that he only needs one more wooden leg and he'll be a table. Good for playing cards on!' The barman guffawed, enjoying sharing the comment with new listeners and, in warm good humour, shook his head at them all. He stood, knuckles on his hips, and watched the old man's slow arrival.

The barman directed the new arrival to the table where Beth and Robert were sitting and pulled out the third chair for him. '*Paolo, siediti qui, per favore*' (Please take a seat here). Paolo nodded, and sat down, waving to his friends to say he would see them later, '*A più tardi!*'.

Beth looked intently at this elderly gentleman who may have seen, may have known her grandfather when he was Captain Selby. Her heart beat faster as she greeted him in the most formal way her Italian permitted. Then, with the help of the Italian-English dictionary, the barman and more coffee, they slowly, painstakingly began to build a bridge with the barber, the former apprentice, who had gone on to become a Master Barber himself, to span both the language gap and the many years.

It very soon became clear that indeed this was Paolo, the young barber's assistant who 60 years previously had helped her grandfather by bringing him a tiny Italian-English dictionary. As this realisation washed over her, Beth stared briefly down at the small tattered book on the simple wooden table in front of her. She could say nothing. Her heart was so full. She felt it might burst.

In the background, at the other side of the piazza, a group of small children were running round and laughing as they played a skipping game. Nearby, an old black dog lay fast asleep on the warm stone of the slabs in the mellow sunshine. Beth glanced up from the dictionary, looked round, and smiled. She became conscious of the sharp and bitter contrast between the gentleness of this peaceful afternoon and the times they were about to discuss. It was all so ordinary, life going on in this quiet Italian backwater.

She frowned to refocus her thoughts on the purpose of this chance, wonderful meeting! Word by word, phrase by phrase, she and Robert started to unravel Paolo's story. It was extraordinary.

Paolo remembered the POW camp. He remembered it well. A glint of excitement and new energy flashed from time to time in his eyes as, over the next hour and with many gestures and much recourse to the little dictionary, he told them his story.

He had been a young lad of not quite 12 when war broke out, and back then throughout his teenage years he was Giovanni the Barber's assistant, later his official apprentice.

The barman brought Paolo a coffee. The old man took a sip, set down his cup and now the story flowed fast. In an intense and hectic whirl of Italian, punctuated by helpful interjections in broken English from the barman and the frantic turning of the fragile pages of the dictionary by Beth, the circumstances of this local lad's connection with the camp emerged.

Even Robert stepped in from time to time with interpretations of the words or phrases, much to Beth's surprise. 'From the Latin.' explained Robert with a shrug, 'Lawyers know a lot of Latin.' Beth smiled. 'Like Dadu!' she thought.

Paolo explained how every so often Giovanni the Barber would be called into the camp to trim the soldiers' hair and give them a professional shave. He needed a helper to support him with so many captive clients, so young assistant Paolo would go too. He told them how he was very excited to be able to go into 'il Campo' – the POW camp – especially the first time. He swept up the hair, prepared and cleaned the razors, washed the combs – and sometimes he got to comb through hair before the barber himself did the cutting.

Paolo added that his bag was unusually heavy on the days when they visited the POW camp because he took more in than hairbrushes. The old man looked at Beth and Robert, and winked before he continued. He leant forward, as if to emphasise that an important moment in the story had arrived. Beth and Robert instinctively leant forward too.

'You see, there was a big game going on. The Red Cross made up parcels for the POWs and sometimes these were dropped in boxes with parachutes by British aircraft. Some were collected officially and delivered, but others went off track. These were fair game for whichever side got to them first – us or the Germans! Well, I was a young, fast lad who could crawl through hedges and climb over walls to run into the fields. So I was recruited on those evenings by the partisans to help. My job was to cut off the parachute straps and collect the parcels before the Nazi vehicles could get there. I would drag as much of the contents as possible to the road, then the partisans would quickly split the boxes into small bundles, one for each rider and we all ran or cycled home. There was a curfew at night, so we could not afford to be caught. Later, we all used our jobs at the camp or our contacts with the Italian soldiers as a way to deliver the goods, or at least most of them, to the men.' Paolo's misty old eyes gleamed with a youthful glimmer as he cast his mind back to those adventurous but dangerous nights.

'There were British bombers too and we had to keep a sharp eye out for those patrols.'

'Yes, true,' added the barman, 'but the POWs in the camp were safe from attack by their own side, because it was the only place in the area with its lights on!' Paolo laughed in agreement and nodded, as if shaking memories into sharper focus.

Paolo spoke again. 'Why are you asking? Did you know someone who was at the camp?' Beth explained about her grandfather and held up his English-Italian pocket dictionary. She was about to add more, '*Mio nonno*,' (My grandfather) – but stopped when she saw Paolo's reaction to the sight of the little book. It was only now that he looked at it closely for the first time.

The barber had sat bolt upright. His bushy eyebrows shot upwards, pushing deep folds into his crinkled forehead, like ripples on a pond. He rocked back in his chair and let out a grunt of surprise and delight. '*Il Ragioniere!*' The Accountant! He exclaimed, then waved his stick at his old pals. In rapid excited Italian he exclaimed, '*Ecco la nipotina del Ragioniere nel campo!*' (This is the granddaughter of The Accountant from the camp!)

At this, the old pals all started talking and waving their arms or sticks at once. They called to the ever-patient waiter and ordered wine for both tables. Then, with much more discussion, confusion and risk of falling over, they got up and pushed the tables together.

Beth and Robert sat enthralled. They exchanged excited glances – but were not quite able to believe that they seemed to have exceeded their most ambitious hopes and might actually have found someone who had known the POWs and even met Reg himself. Beth felt overwhelmed and deeply grateful that she had decided to make this trip to visit Fontanellato for herself, thanks in large part to Robert's suggestion.

While the barman brought the wine and glasses, and the group of old and new friends settled around the rearranged tables. She gathered her thoughts as fast as she could. What else should she ask? What else might he know? Which questions would or could trigger the memories that would tie together the threads in her grandfather's notes?

Meanwhile the barman, now beaming with a broad grin, brought a tray of bottles of the local *rosso*. He poured the rich dark liquid into the array of waiting *bicchiere*, the typical glass tumblers and the men handed them round. The wine was almost blackcurrant in colour and flavour, slightly *frizzante* and Beth found, as it slipped warmly down her throat, utterly delicious. She felt herself lost in thought for a moment, imagining the vineyard where the grapes might have grown, where her grandfather may have sheltered and where he found life-saving help.

The band of friends were about to take a drink when one of them realised they should make a toast. Instantly, a rather too lively discussion began on who or what to toast, until the barman intervened. 'What's this all about now?' he asked, waving his hands in the air and landing them firmly back on their usual resting place on both broad hips.

Beth blushed and felt a little embarrassed that she had already taken a sip. Robert whispered to her the suggestion that they tactfully toast their hosts and Beth quickly raised her glass and said, '*A voi*! To you all!' This compromise was readily accepted by the group, keen to get started on the wine and they returned the favour with a loud, '*A voi*' so that the drinking – and more talking – could start in earnest.

Paolo explained. 'The first time that I went into *il Campo* to help the master barber cut the prisoners' hair, there was one particular young *Inglese* with very blue eyes. I could not help noticing because they were so bright and so blue! I remember that he watched me quite intently, as if he wanted to communicate with me. I was sweeping up around him, wondering what a British soldier would have to say to someone like me. Then he greeted me quietly in Italian. He smiled and looked kind. I wanted to help him – he was a prisoner, after all. He seemed like a clever man, so I looked out for something to bring for him the next time we came to do the POWs' hair. We did not get any food in the next drop, so I took what I could.

The next time I saw him, I offered to comb through his hair and the barber nodded that I could. I opened my heavy brush-bag and slid an English book onto his lap hidden under the towel. The English soldier nodded and tucked it into his shirt, but he whispered, '*Grazie. Ancora?*'

'That's "Thank you, er… more?" ' the barman interjected, 'So you see,' he said to Beth with a grin, 'your grandpa, he wanted more!' The barman and Beth both smiled together – a moment of shared understanding at the thought of the young soldier's resilience, even as a prisoner.

'The next time I had parcels to smuggle in,' Paolo continued, 'I brought him a small English and Italian dictionary.' With a dramatic pause Paolo reached over and gently took the small battered book from Beth's hands. He held it, stroked it, and brushed a tear from his eye. Everyone fell silent as they all seemed to feel the significance of this extraordinary moment – now, here in the piazza, in the fading afternoon of this restful day – a moment in the lives of these people from such different generations, countries and backgrounds, brought together by this extraordinary shared history.

Paolo silently handed the little book back to Beth, and drank his red wine down in one. 'Francesco, *per favore!*' The barman quietly refilled the empty glass. Paolo sat silently for a moment, then looked up at Beth and, stabbing the air with his finger to emphasise his story, took up his tale once more.

'By then, everyone at the camp was calling him The Accountant, *Il Ragioniere!*' Paolo's pals repeated this like the echo of a chorus to his tale. 'I heard that was because he spent his days studying the bookkeeping handbook from the Red Cross. If he would do that while he was in a concentration camp in Italy, I felt sure that he would put in the time to learn Italian too – and that made me very happy.'

Paolo stretched out a trembling hand again to touch the warped and faded dictionary. He looked at Beth, the granddaughter of the young *Inglese* with the blue eyes. Now his own eyes once again brimmed with tears – tears that welled from a deep sense of pride and gratitude to know that all their risks and efforts so many years ago had been worthwhile. They, the people of Fontanellato, had made a difference.

Beth was delighted. Here was confirmation. 'So you met him – when he was here!' Beth's dark eyes were sparkling and her curls swayed as she leant forward, keen to hear more, 'Do you know what happened after that?'

Paolo frowned and shook his head. *'Mi dispiace.'* (I am very sorry), 'I can only tell you that he left the camp when the guards opened the gates. You probably know that on the 8th of September 1943 – everyone here remembers that date,' all the other older men nodded, 'Italy changed sides in the war. The Italian officers at the camp thought that they should give the British a chance. So on the 9th, they opened the gates. I think that most of the officers left that day. But we heard that many were captured and sent to Germany. Some were certainly killed by the Nazis who soon arrived in tanks and armoured cars to round them up. But

I never saw *Il Ragioniere* again. I was sad about that. I liked him.' Paolo paused, his eyes somewhere else, seeing scenes and people in the long gone past. But then added with a smile, 'Ha! So the smart man made it home in the end!'

He raised his glass again as if in tribute, took a sip and then a longer draught. He savoured it for a moment, looking into the almost empty glass as if it too were filled with memories from the distant past. Then, with a look of clear satisfaction, 'You know, I think that the dictionary helped him! There were other soldiers who escaped, but they did not know Italian. Two were caught at the railway station. It would be a funny story, but it is not, because they did not get away. They were seen going into the ladies' toilet by mistake – you see,' he said, leaning forward and moving his lips very broadly to explain the point, 'it is *signore* for women but *signori* for men! Someone saw them make this mistake and reported it, so they were soon recaptured. There were lots of jokes about that amongst the villagers. Those two officers were referred to as 'the ladies' for a long time after that!' Then he frowned and some of the other faces around the table were suddenly cast down, 'Of course the term 'ladies' was just used to lighten the mood. Their mistake cost them their lives. They were executed.' He hesitated for the significance of this to strike home. 'But the message was clear. Other escapees and helpers had to be more careful. You see, The Accountant, he had realised that already!' This was a great excuse for them all to mumble hearty agreement and raise their glasses again.

Beth smiled and she felt sure that Paolo was right. The little Italian dictionary had helped save her grandfather's life and she looked at his time-worn, grinning face with the warmth of deep gratitude. The mist of memory drifted into the eyes of the assembled friends as they each followed the remembered impressions to times and places that had meant so much in their youth. Beth closed her eyes and listened to the sounds around her. The gentle hubbub of voices around the other tables in the café, the bark of a dog in the distance and the peals of children's laughter echoing around from the other side of the castle.

Robert shifted in his seat. He could see that Beth was feeling engulfed by the emotional impact of this powerful chance encounter and was keen to help her learn more before the wine clouded these already fading memories any further. He took a breath and leaned towards Paolo. 'Do you know where the other men went when they escaped?' he asked.

After a rough translation, the reply came from Paolo. 'That's a good question,' he said jabbing his index finger energetically across the table. 'The ones who were caught had mainly headed south to try to meet the arriving Allies – but unfortunately those forces had a hard fight to work their way up through Italy. I heard some escapees walked over 100 miles and many did not reach their comrades, though a few of course did get through in the end.'

'Perhaps The Accountant had other plans,' one of Paolo's companion's suggested. He turned to Beth. 'Maybe your grandfather had heard that partisans were based on higher ground and headed for the hills. They are southwest of here. The headquarters at that time was near the village of Pellegrino Parmense, near Salsomaggiore.'

Then another of the old men added. 'And Varano Marchesi. Some of the soldiers went there too.'

Paolo raised his bushy grey eyebrows and nodded. '*Sì! Giusto!*' (Right!) 'And Varano Marchesi,' he confirmed and took another sip of his wine.

Along the table, another of the men leant forward, 'My family helped five Englishmen to escape!' he said, opening his eyes wide and raising his glass again, but finding it rather low on wine, held it out for an old friend to fill again.

'That's Antonio, the cheesemaker,' explained the barman, who was just passing with a tray of drinks for another table. Then Antonio added, shaking his head, 'I'm afraid your grandfather wasn't one of them.'

A third compatriot, already ruddy in the face, right to the tip of his round ears with the warmth of the wine, now joined in and asked, 'Do you have any names? Sometimes the escapees kept a record of the families they had stayed with and wrote down the number of days that they stayed in each home. I think they hoped the British Government would pay them back for their hospitality after the war.'

'Yes, Giorgio,' added another, rather slumped in his chair and staring into his empty glass as if hoping it would refill itself. 'Pity the British were broke when the war ended and the compensation, if we got it, was small,' he said, then looked up, eyes twinkling with a new thought, 'My father wanted a new tractor but only got enough for one wheel!' the old pals let out peals of laughter again at the thought of each family getting a shiny new red British tractor for keeping soldiers fed on polenta and hidden in haylofts.

'He probably spent a few days with Filomena Scaglioni,' said Paolo, 'Many of the young escapees stopped at her house before they were placed with families. Very brave lady!'

'Hoo! Quite a force of nature!' said Antonio, flicking his fingers as if to under-line his words, 'Mind you, she had to flee in the end, once the *Fascisti* started to suspect.' Murmurs of agreement led to the raising of yet another toast, this time to the women of the war in the villages, who kept everything going and, they said, were just as brave as the men.

Beth flicked through the documents in her large folder she had brought with her, looking for a small scrap of lined paper with Italian words and numbers on it. 'Are these names?' she asked, showing Paolo the sheet. He stared but could not focus and they all laughed again as they handed the paper round trying to find someone who had remembered their reading glasses.

The barman took the sheet. He looked at the paper and hesitated. 'Is this from your *nonno*?' he asked. Beth nodded to the barman and immediately, the group of friends became alert again. The barman fished his spectacles out of his pocket and balanced them on the end of his large nose as he read aloud from the handwritten list. The names were arranged in a column:

Chiesa, Domenico	112
Esterra	42
Erminia	21
Spotti	15
Aldina	15
Sabani	12
Musile, Paroletta, others	10
Total	227

'Spotti?' said one shaky voice. Several of the men crossed themselves and the atmosphere changed. It was suddenly as if all the threads of shared experience that tied these folk together had just pulled a little tighter.

Beth looked from one to the other, but the old men stayed silent, eyes lowered, as if the mention of the name had led them away to a shadowy corridor, from which they would not easily return.

The barman answered gently instead. 'Yes, they are names of families that helped the escapees. Some of their stories did not have a happy ending.' He shook his head, as if shaking off that harsh reality. Beth and Robert looked at one another, unsure how to continue, but the barman was there to help. 'So I think the numbers are days. The days that he lived with each of them. It looks as if he spent the longest time with the Chiesa family. Perhaps you can go to the villages and find them. Maybe someone there can tell you more!'

'No, Francesco. They will all be long gone! Like our parents! It's only us left now,' said Antonio, and the group nodded.

Then Giorgio, a little younger than the others, suggested, 'At least go to the cemeteries. They have the dates and photos on the grave plaques, so you can see who survived the war – huh! And the warlike peace that followed here in *Italia*.' The old comrades murmured agreement to this and waved a hand here and there as if to brush away the bad memories of the troubles that followed the war.

The mention of graves seemed to close the conversation. At last the talk of the past – of parents, neighbours, of the stories and the old photographs – led them back to a different place and time. Each one of them appeared to have left the table already in their minds. Beth thanked them all and closed her folder too.

The sun, now softening as the afternoon drew on, bathed the castle walls in a muted orange sheen. Most of the other tables had emptied and even the black dog had sauntered away. It felt like they had reached the natural conclusion of this amazing but chance encounter.

Beth looked across at Paolo with a mixture of gratitude and affection as, one by one, the friends prepared to depart. Paolo shook Beth and Robert's hands, then pushed two-handed on his walking stick to lever his weary body up from the chair and shift his weight onto his good foot. He nodded and smiled towards Beth and Robert. 'I wish you many sons!' he said.

Taken aback, Beth wanted to protest that she and Robert were not a couple but, instead, with a stark red blush across her face, managed to smile back. Then with a shake of her auburn hair, she collected herself and stood up to thank him again. With an uncharacteristic flush of emotion, Beth stepped forward and gave him a hug. Paolo chuckled, surprised and a little embarrassed, but inwardly delighted. Then he shook Robert by the hand again and set off back across the square.

Beth and Robert watched in silence. The old friends waved and called their last greetings as they each headed homeward in various directions. While the barman cleared the tables and stacked the chairs away, the English couple stood mesmerised, trying, it seemed, to grasp if the meeting they had just shared was really a dream. They kept watching as Paolo shuffled slowly back across the *piazza*, appearing to fade into the worn old stones as he passed out of sight.

⁓ — ⁓

Back at the hotel restaurant, Robert was in a bright mood. 'What jolly chaps!' he said, reflecting on the day, as they waited for their *risotto* with local parmesan cheese. 'Yes,' Beth agreed, but she was distracted. Something from today's conversation was connected to another document, but she could not remember which one. She sat at the table scribbling notes to capture all that they had heard, while Robert chatted on, trying to entertain and lighten her spirits.

He had a great way of telling stories about his family holidays in Italy with a dry but tender humour. Every tale depicted a similar pattern of his father's ambitious and stylish plans brought to nought by the antics of this accident-prone son. He told of deflating lilos sinking under his mother in the pool, of lost hotel room keys causing havoc in Sorrento, embarrassing trips to the British Embassy with flambéed passports or whatever disaster may have occurred – the cause of which could somehow always be traced back to him.

Eventually, Beth put her pen and papers aside and just smiled at him. He had an irresistible way of charming the stress from her with his wild tales. 'So how did you end up working for him?' she asked playfully, 'Having seen what happened to keys and passports, how come he was prepared to let you loose on his valuable clients?'

'Ah, well,' said Robert, nervously passing a hand through his smooth, dark blond hair, 'he didn't have a choice. You see he prided himself on employing the best. He placed an advert at my law school saying that his firm would take on that year's top student in the exams.'

'What? And that was you?' asked Beth, incredulous.

'Thanks! You didn't need to sound so surprised! You see, I've been drowning in law conversations at home since I was in primary school. I might have struggled to finish a knickerbocker glory without accidentally flicking a strawberry across the restaurant, but when it came to passing exams, I knew the case names, dates and references as well as I knew my own address.'

'Do you get on with your father now?'

'Yes, in general. We just don't go skiing together anymore. But how his favourite skis fell off the cable car into the deepest valley at the resort honestly had nothing to do with me…'

Beth could not repress a giggle. But this time, her glance at him was honed with a new respect. He was a smart lawyer after all – just a clumsy one.

At the end of the meal, they decided to take an evening walk. Robert and Beth went to the gates to look more closely at the plaque on the pillar by the main entrance, commemorating its time as a World War II prisoner-of-war camp, *Campo di Concentramento PG 49* and its role in the conflict. They walked the quiet, peaceful streets in the fading sun. It seemed unimaginable to think of this place rattled by the sound of marching boots and rolling tanks. She looked around the scene as if searching in it for a clue.

'Which way would you go?' commented Robert, 'I mean, if you were a prisoner with no maps who had never been outside the camp since the day you were brought here, which way would you go?'

'Good question,' said Beth, thoughtful. 'Let's think. So, you come out of the camp gates here. You know you have to get away before the Germans arrive and you're caught and shot, because you're not in full uniform, you're wearing a mixture of uniform and Red Cross recycled clothes. There are no road signs and you have no maps. You don't know which direction you arrived from because you were in a closed truck. Your only guide is the sun, I suppose.'

She looked up at the golden light fading on the horizon. 'That way is west, so southwest is over there,' she said, pointing. 'Let's see.' They walked down the street that led in that general direction as far as the edge of the town and looked out across the fields in the dusk. The dark outline of the trees gave way to low hedges and vineyards. In the distance, a wavy indigo band stretched across the horizon, silhouetted against the darkening sky – the distant hills. 'And soon it will be night with no food and nowhere to sleep.'

'Paolo said that the partisans were in the hills over there. If Reg knew that, then maybe this is the road he would have chosen,' said Robert. Beth shivered despite the warmth of the evening air and looked across the open landscape. In her head she could hear the regular fast thudding of two men in heavy boots as they panted hard – unfit from many months of incarceration and short rations – and tried to settle into a steady pace. They needed to keep going for many hours. It was summer for her now but for them it would have been autumn. Shorter days and cooler nights.

'Shall we go back to the hotel?' asked Robert, noticing that she had suddenly crossed her arms, clutching and rubbing the bare skin as if against the cold. She nodded, trying to shake off the inner chill she had suddenly felt and they headed back in silence.

＠ — ＠

When Robert came down to the lobby in the morning, Beth was already there. 'I got your text asking me to come down quickly,' he said holding up his phone as if to prove it. 'Have you found something out?'

'Not yet,' she said. 'But Paolo and his café comrades were right. We need to follow his trail and go to the hills. We need to go to the village of Pellegrino Parmense. The taxi is here. I'll tell you on the way.'

'No breakfast?'

'Later, Robert. Apparently it's *Parmigiano* festival time, so we can eat something there.'

'Of course! The festival! Parmesan cheeses, honey and wine. There's a notice in the hotel lobby. Now that's a breakfast I could get used to!'

'Ach, Robert!'

In the taxi, Beth explained that in her sleep, her thoughts had been re-assembling the pieces. The words *Chiesa* and *Domenico* were chasing each other around in her mind and kept landing on a piece of paper that then blew away.

That morning, when she had woken up, she was sure that the next step had something to do with those two words: *Chiesa* and *Domenico*. They had not only been written on the list that the barman had read out yesterday. They were also written on a sealed envelope in the suitcase marked on the back as 'Private'. *Domenica*, spelt with a final 'A', means Sunday. Here, the word was spelt with an 'o' – *Domenico*. But it was very similar and since *Chiesa* means church, she had thought that the two words were the name of a place. She had been puzzled as to why the note would be there at all, but since it had seemed to be something to do with 'church', she had respected what she thought were her grandfather's wishes and left it sealed. Now she questioned her assumption and had brought the letter down with her. She explained to Robert as she turned the envelope over and over in her hands that yesterday the men at the café had said that *Domenico* is a person's first name. *Chiesa* is a family name – so *Domenico Chiesa* was a person on his list of hosts in the area. The letter must be about that person.

The list had said Domenico Chiesa, 112 so Beth had finally realised what had been puzzling her. Reg must have spent 112 days being hidden by his family. So Domenico had helped her grandfather for the longest time of all the families – nearly four months. That family had kept him fed, housed and safe in those dangerous days, weeks and months. That changed everything. Perhaps the message did not mean 'don't open it,' but rather 'this document contains confidential information, so has been sealed separately.' Perhaps she should open it after all. The letter was with the rest of the papers that she had received in the suitcase, so it was there for her to read. Suddenly it felt vital to know what was inside.

As they sped along winding roads, getting closer to that wavy line of distant hills, Beth held up the marked envelope in her hand and looked to Robert for approval in taking the next step deeper into her grandfather's story.

'Shall I?' she asked.

'Go ahead. Remember, if anything bad happens, it's okay, because you have a lawyer with you!'

Beth smiled. He may be an unconventional helper, but he was right. The message was clear:

> You've come this far and perhaps you do need to know what you might meet at the next step on the journey.

She slipped a pencil under the flap and the old adhesive easily gave way and then the envelope was open. The sheets inside were of very thin paper, closely written as if each page had very special value. Whatever they were about to discover, her grandfather had had a lot to tell.

> These notes are sealed separately from the rest of my report out of respect for the feelings of my wife of many years. Though I met my wife after the war was long since over, the contents of these pages could perhaps cause her unnecessary pain.
>
> After a few days of being moved from safe-house to safe-house, some in Varano Marchesi and other villages, I spent the most time in Pellegrino Parmense, where I went to live with the Chiesa family. The brave parents had accepted the risk to their lives and those of their three children, two sons and a daughter, to protect a British stranger. While it was still night, I was taken to their house by the partisans and they welcomed me in. That is when I first saw Maria…

As Beth read on, a picture was painting itself with each new line. She was journeying into the most precious secret of her grandfather's wartime past. He was now sharing with her a secret that even Nanna, his wife of so many decades knew nothing about. She, his granddaughter, was to be the keeper of this story and in this letter, perhaps, he was about to open another part of his heart.

As their car climbed to around 600 metres, the village road was decorated with bunting and announcements of the Summer Cheese Festival, the *Fiera del Parmigiano-Reggiano di Montagna* in Pellegrino Parmense. This was always held in July and was separate from the later, September festival.

At the top of a long winding ascent, they were almost at the entrance to the village when they spotted a café. 'Let's stop here and ask. It seems full of villagers already!' suggested Robert.

They left the taxi and walked over to the door which, though open, was shielded from insects by the long beaded tassels of a traditional fringe curtain. The sound of many intertwined, enthusiastic conversations laced with laughter, spilled out into the morning sun.

Beth gently parted the beaded fronds and entered first. The café was almost completely full, mainly with older residents, perhaps keen to avoid the hustle and noise of the festival in the village streets down the hill. Robert, her tall, blond companion followed, blocking out the sunlight for a moment as he entered the crowded room. The loud hubbub in the bar fell instantly silent. Beth hesitated for a moment, then she walked from table to table asking if the vacant seats were free, but all were barred with an arm or the barked word '*occupato!*' – taken! The formerly happy faces of the villagers, many of whom were clearly older residents from the area, frowned and turned away. Robert and Beth glanced at each other, but made their way across the café to a corner table where at last, a couple allowed them to sit down by simply not replying to her request.

A long wait followed. The waiter appeared deliberately to miss seeing her raised hand and to avoid walking past their table. Finally, Beth began a conversation in her broken but improving Italian with the woman of the married couple sitting next to her. 'Excuse me, but we are looking to find some people who helped my grandfather. Or, the children or grandchildren of those families.' She explained that her grandfather was a British soldier who was a *prigioniero di guerra* in World War II in Fontanellato. Local people had helped him to escape.

Robert meanwhile sat quiet, sensing the frosty atmosphere. He was not very comfortable – and he was hungry. The honey-and-cheese breakfast he had been looking forward to was taking rather too long to appear. He turned to Beth to see if he could help as she struggled to find the right words to deal with this new and unfamiliar situation. However, he noticed straight away how her Italian had already improved with the practice of the previous day's conversations. As he watched, he saw how the husband of the woman Beth was talking to at the table gradually began to listen in as well. He saw the old man slowly turn to focus more closely on what she was saying. He frowned.

'*Inglese?*' he asked suddenly.

'*Sì!* Yes English'

'*Anche lui?*' (him too?) he asked, indicating Robert with a twitch of his head.

'Yes, he's English too – *sì, anche lui*' Beth replied.

'*Non è Tedesco?*' (He's not German?) Came the incredulous reply.

'*È Inglese,*' he's English, she confirmed.

As if a firework had gone off beneath him, the old man and his large stomach burst out from behind the table. All of a sudden, he stood up, began speaking fast and loudly, gesticulating towards the barman in energetic support of his words.

The ribbons of his phrases unfurled around the room. They flew, linking the guests at every table and reaching out to the barman and his wife behind the counter. Each person they touched broke into wide smiles and rapid excited chatter. In an instant, the café was once again full of noise and voices, as each exclaimed at the newcomers' identity, '*Inglesi!*' '*La nipotina*,' '*La Guerra*.' People rose from their chairs to gather round the small corner table where Beth and Robert were sitting, keen to be part of the news of the day.

Beth looked around, wide-eyed. Then, catching snatches of conversation that consisted mainly of '*Inglesi, Inglesi!*', it dawned on her – something Robert had already realised. 'Oh my goodness, Robert! They thought you were German, or, or Nazi, and that's why they did not welcome us! Now they know we're here to thank them for their wartime support of us as Brits, they're excited to help! Wow! We really *are* in partisan territory!'

Robert shifted uneasily in his seat and blinked his grey-blue eyes. 'Well, I'm glad you feel good about it!' he said. 'For a moment there I thought I might be in for a right parmesan lynching!'

Soon faces and bodies were pressed close to the backs of their chairs, leaning over the table. Tumblers of wine and coffee, cognac and sweet pastries appeared in front of them and questions swirled around in the air above their heads.

'Who are you looking for?'

'Which families helped?'

'When was this?'

'Did the soldier survive?'

'Of course he survived, *idiota* – she is his granddaughter!'

'What was his name?'

'Did I know him?'

'Well *did* you?'

'Listen, lady, we can help. Just tell us who you are looking for!'

Beth looked around at all the expectant faces and slowly, with the help of Robert, began in her halting, simple Italian. 'My grandfather was Lieutenant, later Captain Reginald Selby. He stayed with a number of families in these hills. The longest time was with the Chiesa family. We are looking for information about them. There were two sons and a daughter, Maria.'

Glances were exchanged as they thought about the new information. 'Ah. *Chiesa, Domenico. Sai?*' Do you know him?

'*Chiesa, sì,* I know that family. *Ma Maria?*' – but Maria?

'*Aspetta*' – wait, said the barman, wiping his hands on his apron. He reached for a well-thumbed telephone directory. 'I have the old names.'

'Chiesa… Chiesa… Maria Chiesa, I think she works in a factory over the hill.'

'No, she is not married but her friend is that chap…'

And so the morning ran on.

At last, Beth and Robert emerged through the beaded curtain, much the worse for local wine, but not much the wiser, except to know how deeply the older villagers still felt about the past, how they had supported the British troops – and how ready everyone still was to help where they could.

With much thanking and waving, Beth and the English lawyer blinked and stepped gingerly along the path down the hill into the village. They walked, as if through an unreal dreamscape, past the bunting, stalls and barrels of the wine at the cheese and honey festival and into the growing sounds of jubilation down in Pellegrino Parmense. Beth's head was dizzy, not just with the effects of the wine early in the day, but from the intensity of the experience. The strength of feelings, both negative and positive, the energy and the generosity were all overwhelming.

As they wandered past the stalls, a sense of normality gradually returned. They bought some cheese and then one of the last remaining fresh loaves. There were dried meats, sliced thin and delicious with tiny tasty samples presented on wooden platters to 'try-before-you-buy'. Music played in the background so that all the senses were accosted and entangled in this festival – the warmth of the sun, the smells of the wares, the taste of the succulent morsels and the wondrous sights of the colourful displays.

It felt good to see this village in happy times, times of peace and plenty. Some of the shops would have changed hands, but most of the buildings were old enough to be the same as they had been during the war years. She wondered how much her Dadu had seen of this place and what it had meant to him in those strange and difficult months.

7

Maria

The threat of war, the hope of peace
The Kingdom's peril and increase
Sleep on and bide the latter day
When fate shall take her chain away

William Morris, *Verses to accompany The Legend of the Briar Rose,*
a set of paintings by Edward Burne-Jones – Painting two, The Council Room

There was just the smallest sliver of moon on that warm autumn night, like a slender *falcetto* blade carving a sickle slice of light in the dark sky.

The side door of the farming home was draped in the misshapen shadows of wall-climbing red trumpet campsis, weaving and turning as if to interrogate the arriving stranger with sharp-angled looks. To the lad from Hertfordshire, son of a gardener, the exotic Mediterranean bells and the perfumes of night jasmine flooded his senses with almost overwhelming intensity. He pressed his back to the wall behind his partisan guide, breathed in the air heady with glorious aromas of the night garden. Then the door opened and the gentle golden light of a single candle lit the doorway.

The farmer, Signor Domenico Chiesa leant forward, hand outstretched in welcome. He had an open face with dark but bright eyes, a noble nose and a thick but well-trimmed dark moustache that arched over his ready smile. A dimple appeared on one side like an exclamation mark for each happy thought. *'Buona sera! Benvenuto!'* (Good evening, welcome), he whispered.

As they stepped swiftly inside, his wife bustled over from the kitchen, wiping her hands on her apron and pushing back a wayward curl of slightly greying dark hair. She nodded and smiled as her husband introduced the stranger.

Their two sons, Guido and Gianni – short for Giovanni – came forward to be presented in turn. They were only about 20 and 18 respectively but were already developing strong farm hands and broad backs in the hard work of the fields.

Like many in the remoter parts, they had so far avoided being called up. They nodded at the blond, blue-eyed soldier who stood smart and erect, if unkempt, in front of them. It was the first foreigner they had seen and they simply stared. Domenico waved his hand and they stepped aside, moving lightly back to make way for their younger sister, perhaps 16 or 17, who entered with a plate of freshly baked *biscotti* (biscuits).

She moved calmly and smoothly in a heavily embroidered skirt, which swung with the measured sway of damask. Her black, thick wavy hair rolled carelessly over her smooth shoulders and when she shyly glanced up at the Englishman, the sparkles in her deep brown eyes took his breath away. 'My daughter, Maria,' said Signor Chiesa.

Keen to make a good impression on the new host family, and particularly on the wonderful Maria, but unsure how to start, Reg chose the safe bet of offering his military title. 'Lieutenant Reginald Edward Selby, Bedfordshire and Hertfordshire 2nd Regiment, C Company, at your service!' He said it in English, then saluted Maria smartly. She blushed at the formality of the introduction, so Reg quickly added a small bow and, reaching out a hand took one of the delicious *biscotti* from the tray. With a quick glance up at her with his bright blue eyes, he added an Italian phrase – '*Con molto piacere!*' (With great pleasure!)

Maria giggled and the partisan slapped Reg on the shoulder playfully. 'You English gentlemen!' he joked, 'If only your charms worked so well on the Nazis! Now, Selby, I leave you with good people, so remember what I said. Their lives are in your hands as much as yours lies in theirs.'

Reg nodded, the playful smile quickly dissolving into a frown that matched the responsibility here being accepted by both sides. The partisan held out his hand which Reg gratefully took and shook warmly. In the best, most correct Italian he could muster, he said, 'Thank you. I shall remember. And I am ready to help you whenever you need me.'

'In the meantime,' said Signor Chiesa, 'you are very welcome. But, I warn you, everyone has to earn their dinner here! You can help in the kitchen during the day and after dark, go to fetch water from the well in the small courtyard, ready for the morning. You can bring in a supply of firewood from the stack for the hearth and whatever else needs doing. Don't worry, you'll still be available to go out with the partisans on raids whenever they need reinforcements with military experience.' Reg had only caught about half the words, but understood the gist well enough. Just be helpful. He nodded.

'Finish your *biscotti* and I'll show you round,' said the elder brother, Guido.

He took Reg to his own room, where a straw mattress and some blankets were laid out. Reg would share that space for now. The lavatory was outside of course, but he should wash inside the room with a bowl of water, to minimise the risk of anyone seeing him.

In the back room, Gianni picked up the corner of a rug on the floor. He showed Reg a trap door underneath, leading to a small overflow cellar. If the Nazis came calling, Reg would need to hurry here and slide inside. It was just big enough for a man to crawl into, between the bottles of wine and stored parmesan cheeses. '*Ecco*, here you are,' he said, 'if there is a *Rastrellamento,* that is if the German soldiers come looking for you, this is where you hide, silent, still and praying as hard as you can for all our safety.' He crossed himself and pressed his hands together. Reg searched for the right vocabulary and his weak Italian gave way to school Latin. '*Deo volente*, God willing,' he said. And his new, Catholic brother echoed the well-worn words. '*Sì. Deo volente.'*

Maria's light, tapping steps on the old tiles interrupted their exchange. She entered the small room, bringing a bright smile and on her outstretched arms, the spare set of clothes that they had hurriedly put together from her brothers' outfits. Reg held them up to his frame. The sleeves of the jacket were too short and the trouser legs stopped mid-calf. Gianni laughed, Maria giggled again and she and the tall, fair guest shared a warm smile.

8

Captive Freedom

Man works till set of sun,
A woman's work is never done!
Anon

The partisans found clothes to fit Reg and a daily routine fell into place. He got up before dawn when the family rose, and completed his chores. He pumped water from the well in the yard and brought it into the kitchen. He restocked the stack of firewood by the kitchen stove from the piles of brushwood in the yard outside, fed the chickens and took food scraps to the family's pig before joining the family for breakfast.

After that was done, the days were long. The menfolk were out working the land and there was little in the house that he was allowed to do. He sat in the warm kitchen amongst the wonderful smells of herbs drying on hooks hung from the ceiling and watched Maria and her mother kneading dough for bread, preparing the maize for *polenta* or boiling up great vats of soup from chicken bones and vegetables to feed the hungry family.

The better-off farming families were often politically close to the Fascists and so were on the side of the former government. They took in few if any POWs and there was little trust in their discretion. The poorer families were often peasant farmers, *mezzadri* who worked the land without owning it, but their allegiance was simple – to all people in need – and they shared their crust, however meagre, with whoever was hungry and whatever the risk.

At home, he had never appreciated the skill and planning that goes into running the household. Now he understood better the work of these busy women and loved watching them, especially the bright-eyed Maria. She liked to snatch glances at him too and gradually became more trusting and more playful. On washdays he helped in carrying out the heavy, wet bed linen to hang on the lines. She waited until he was weighed down with the damp cloth then flicked washing water at him, secure that he could not respond. At first he simply played along.

Then he got wise. He appeared to ignore her splashes and hung out the large sheets but did not come back inside. Curious, she crept behind the sheets and he quickly wrapped her in the damp cloth, twisting her round inside so she could not easily escape. She squealed and laughed, pleased that he had played along and secretly happy that he had won the game.

Home stayed on his mind and Marina, Maria's mother, one day noticed that Reg looked sad as he stood in the open barn sharpening the sickle and other tools ready for the menfolk to use. Reg was thinking of his father's tools for his work in the gardens and felt a pang of sadness and guilt that he could not tell his own family that he was alright.

Marina called to her daughter, 'Look! He's probably homesick. Go and bring him in. We'll put him to work kneading the dough and making the polenta for dinner. That will take his mind off things.' Maria smiled with delight. She ran across and gently touched Reg on the shoulder. Surprised, he looked down into her trusting, bright eyes that shone with affection. He let her take him by the hand and drag him, half at a run into the kitchen. 'That's too easy for you!' she called, 'You need to do some proper work – women's work!' she teased.

Together, the women taught him to knead the large dollops of thick dough and roll them into shape, ready to cook in the *forno* (oven). It was a strange sort of oven on stilts. Such acts of kindness helped him to feel part of this family, a new family and the good, wholesome food soon rebuilt his strength and energy. The household tasks were welcome, but they seemed very little in return for the risks the family were taking on his behalf. His command of Italian was improving rapidly now that he was completely immersed in the language and he wanted to do more.

After the first month in their protection, thoughts of the regiment and the wider war outside the cocoon of this Italian village began to play on his mind. There was no contact with England, no plans to get home, and no real possibility of making plans to get home. He soon began to feel useless to both his hosts and to the wider war effort. He was not really safe here and the family were taking a huge risk, yet he was barely able to contribute. This was a captive freedom indeed. He felt ready to do more. The next evening, he spoke to Domenico and begged to be allowed to use his renewed strength to support the family in the fields. Eventually, the father agreed. They would say that he was working as a distant cousin, come to help out.

He joined the brothers eagerly in their tasks and was allocated the task of hoeing the land, *zappare*, but it was quickly clear that the soft skin on his hands would not take the strain. They found some old working gloves and he put them on. But there was a problem. The other farmhands did not wear gloves. They got in the way and work was not as efficient. The villagers' hands were like leather, tanned and hardened over many years. At lunchtime, three men from the neighbouring land joined them and they sat together to eat. One of the labourers saw Reg take off his gloves and looked closer at his fine fingers. 'It seems your cousin is not used to farm work,' he commented through a mouthful of cheese. 'Those are not the hands of a farmer. What is he – an accountant?' they all laughed and Signor Chiesa brushed it aside, commenting, 'Something like that!'

This was not going to work. If only one person passed a comment in the village wine bar that the Chiesa family had a fair cousin working with them with hands soft as a girl's, someone would suspect he was an escaped POW and inform. It was too risky.

Conversation over dinner that evening was tense. 'He can't work with us any more, *Papà*,' said the eldest son. 'One slip with his pale hands, one word with his terrible accent and it is not just he who will suffer but us, *Mamma* and Maria too.' Signor Chiesa frowned and his thick moustache wriggled on his top lip, as his mouth twisted, thinking how to reply.

'Shame he has such girly hands!' joked the second son, Gianni, taking another serving of food. 'Then maybe he should be a girl!' giggled Maria.

'You mean dress like a woman?' asked Reg, struggling to follow this new turn in the conversation. They all turned and stared at him.

Then Domenico's moustache stretched out above his fine teeth in a broad grin. 'Yes!' he said, 'Ha! Ha! Why not? We have girl cousins too – and then you can stay away from the rest of the menfolk.'

They all laughed, relieved that a solution had been found and the tension was released. The usual spirit of fun returned. Maria and her mother went in search of female clothes and, to everyone's amusement except Reg's, assembled a suitable outfit, complete with wooden work clogs. Reg stood as an unwilling mannequin to be transformed into a frumpy female cousin. He had to be well covered in drab, loose clothes that reached to the floor to cover his legs and touched the wooden clogs that were rather on the large side for an Italian lady. Soon 'he' could be 'she' and at least do the lighter jobs that would fall to a female – tying and binding, pruning and clearing, fixing and finishing. 'She' worked alongside the ladies, separately from the men, and her rather heavy stature did not draw any admiring glances. This way, the female cousin completed some of the farming tasks. Reg wondered what his younger stepbrother, Victor, would have thought of his petticoats. War hero in lace? He smiled to himself, but was glad to be busy, whatever indignities that might bring. And 'she' could spend more time with Maria, which became an increasing joy and ample compensation for any embarrassments. He could whisper jokes to her while they worked and occasionally even touch her arm, as any affectionate female cousin would naturally do!

The arrival of the late autumn chill signalled that it was time for the annual pig slaughter. The family's one pig would be butchered, processed and preserved in their own kitchen. The cooked meats would be dried, along with smoked sausages to be stored away, eked out to last for the rest of the year. But first, someone had to catch it. This dubious honour was passed to their guest. Reg was invited to doff his underskirts for once, catch and hold the pig in the pen. The pig would be killed with a knife and then hung for exsanguinating before the meat products for the coming year could be prepared.

Since Reg had been feeding the pig every day, he had got to know its moods and felt there would be no problem approaching it and getting a good grip on the animal. He did not count on the intelligence of pigs. The pig immediately sensed a change in the atmosphere when the whole family gathered in front of the pen. Reg climbed in and, instead of just putting down some food and leaving, he came closer. The pig grew nervous, then it grew frightened. Then it ran. It ran round in tight circles, this way and that way, with surprising agility. Reg darted back and forth, grabbing an ear here and a leg there, but not getting a firm hold on this heavy, smart beast, finally almost grasping a shoulder and falling flat in the excrement-ridden mud.

His hosts were fair splitting their sides with laughter as he slithered and grabbed, chased and fell, with the pig all the time squealing and protesting. Finally, the two brothers, faces aching with laughter, took pity on Reg and jumped in to help. With practised skill, they pinned the creature down with the full weight of their two bodies – and the deed could be done.

The well-fatted pig was hung on a hook for its blood to drain out, and the carcass rinsed with buckets of cold water. Reg had to be rinsed too – from matted hair to muddy feet. Maria threw the first bucketful and laughed as he gasped with the shock of the cold dousing. Their eyes met playfully and he flicked mud in her direction. She retaliated with more water and they laughed again. 'I'll take over now, Maria!' said her brother taking the bucket from her hands. Maria retreated to the kitchen, sneaking a backward glance as Reg stripped off the dripping clothes and rubbed himself dry with a cloth.

In the coming days, work on the pig kept the whole family busy. Everyone was involved to make sure the meat was treated while still fresh. Every part was preserved as dried hams and in salamis, so that nothing was wasted. Finally, when these vital supplies were assured for another year, it was time to celebrate.

Marina and Maria prepared a special meal and they all sat down to eat with wine from the cellar under the floor – the rich red wine for once not cut with water. It was accompanied by good cheeses and honey from the village.

Everyone helped prepare for it and Reg took the plates and dishes from Maria to lay on the table. The connection between them was growing stronger by the day and he risked small advances when he saw she was open to them. With the first plate that he took, he made sure their fingers touched. She blushed, but did not pull away. There were many plates and dishes to lay out. The soft fingertips met again and again, out of sight under the rims, and again and again the young hands connected with an electrifying spark.

The meal was the perfect moment to acknowledge the family's success that year – the harvest was in, the pig's meat was secured and the war had not yet taken any souls from amongst their number. There was laughter and relaxation for all.

As the last plates were emptied and cleared away, Maria asked, 'Please let's sing, *Papà*!' *Papà* thought for a moment. He looked at the faces around the table, rosy with the wine and all cheering for a song. His moustache settled into a smile of approval and he fetched his *fisarmonica* (accordion). With the first notes, a new atmosphere settled in the room. The music lifted everyone to a different time and place – back to Sorrento, into the arms of lovers, down to the graveside of loved ones lost, and then out and up into the whirl of new romance. Reg was enthralled. It was so long since he had shared music, which had been an important part of church and community life back home. He listened, determined to learn these new and wonderful melodies and grasp as many of the words as he could.

At last, Domenico asked, 'What about you, Reg, do you sing?'

'Well, I sing in church. And I sing some folk songs,' he ventured. He shot a glance around the room and his eyes settled on the warm and beautiful face of Maria, who smiled encouragingly.

'Go on,' she said, 'Let's hear if you can sing like an Italian!'

The playful challenge was a gauntlet thrown down. Honour was at stake and he simply could not refuse to take it up.

'Alright, here goes.' With thoughts of the hills outside and the green gardens of home, the first song that came into this mind was a haunting, traditional melody. As the first few bars of *Greensleeves* floated into the room, Maria rested her face in her hands to listen.

'Alas, my love, you do me wrong, to cast me off discourteously, for I have loved you so long, delighting in your company…Greensleeves…'

His voice was clear, strong and charged with many emotions. The song drew simultaneously on the feeling of being rejected and away from his homeland, in hiding, and living in a foreign land without the support of his regiment. But it also spoke to his new fascination with the exotic Maria who seemed as lovely and unattainable as home.

He deliberately caught Maria's eye when he sang 'delighting in your company' and, although she did not understand the words, his look and tone made her blush. When he finished the last chorus, there was silence for a second or two, then all the family erupted in applause. Gianni slapped him playfully on the back. So he really could sing! Perhaps he could be a little bit Italian, after all! They would have to teach him all their favourite Italian ballads and there was no time to start like the present. The rest of the evening was a family festival of song. Like two teams in a friendly match of musical exchange, the Italians and the Englishman took it in turns to share the tunes of their traditions, their culture and their hearts. Reg felt accepted, even loved by the family that was now, at last, making him one of their own.

9

Night Raids

Who Dares, Wins.
Who Sweats, Wins.
Who Plans, Wins.

Motto of the Special Air Service, Sir David Stirling,
founder of the SAS in 1940

While romance blossomed in the heart of the family, the war raged on beyond
the hills. Reg and his co-escapee, John Baddeley, were called upon from time to
time, as agreed, to support the partisans. John was being hosted by another brave,
but poor family in the area and accepted many missions during his time with
his hosts. He had been successful in attacks with the rebels, blowing up bridges
needed by the Nazi forces and generally disrupting communications. Italy's
volunteer fighters included many escaping Allied POWs from at least 17 nations,
perhaps over 1,400 of them. The risks were high as nearly 10 percent of those sent
out on raids lost their lives in the area of Emilia-Romagna alone.

On these nights, Reg exchanged his petticoats for the rough, dark clothes he
had used for a while as a male farming cousin. John and the other men were out
more often than Reg, but occasionally they required an extra hand.

Reg was an excellent driver, having learnt to drive many types of vehicles during
his army training back home. He used these skills widely in the months of exercises early in the war – driving trucks, cars and riding motor bikes. It was natural
that his role in this group would be as the driver. The steering may have been new,
and it certainly was strange to be sitting on the left and driving on the other side
of the road. However, the basic skill was the same. Reg soon became familiar with
the back lanes and tracks around the villages and was keen to use his experience to
play his part in these disruptive actions, as a contribution to his protectors.

One night, Reg waited as usual in the dark silent house when all the family
were asleep. A gentle tap on the window was the signal to slip out of the front

door and join the particular raid planned that night. The other men were waiting on a patch of scrub off the lane, close to a nearby farm. Beside them was the truck borrowed from a different farm. If the raiders were captured, the owner would report the truck stolen the next day and so might be allowed to have it back. The farm was dark and silent, so that no suspicion would fall on the family and the presence of the truck would be incidental.

'You are our driver tonight, *Reggio*,' confirmed the commander. 'We're going to disable the transport resources that are kept at the enemy base near Salsomaggiore. We'll set explosives and burn trucks and as many armoured cars as we can.'

'You don't need to worry about right or left-hand drive,' chipped in John. 'The roads are so narrow round here that you can just drive down the middle!' Reg smiled and winked as he climbed into the cab of the truck to familiarise himself with the controls. 'Double-de-clutch. Fine. How long does the choke need to be out?' he asked John, who had climbed in beside him. John shrugged. Reg looked at one of the other partisans, opened his mouth to speak, then realised he had no idea how to explain that question in Italian. He looked back at John and shrugged too. They both grinned and Reg pulled out the choke to start the truck.

The truck wound down the dark lanes, avoiding main roads and at last slowed to a walking pace as they approached the target area. They pulled up and stopped while the engine sound was still out of earshot of any guards that might be patrolling the base. The partisans passed like shadows across the open road to the Nazi headquarters, holding their explosives tight to their bodies in small cloth bags to cushion the sticks of explosives so there was no sound of rattling as they moved. They slipped into the yard and ran along close to the wall, then over to where the vehicles were parked. Reg went through the escape route again in his head, to be ready if they needed to make a fast retreat. He had noticed a rail line with an unfenced level crossing point that was riskier than the route they had taken to reach the base, but which would cut a chunk off their journey and be a quicker shortcut to their familiar backroads, if needed. He repeated the plan to himself to be sure he would turn at the right moment to find it.

The German compound guard was leaning against the wall snoozing, so the *partigiani* were able to file past unnoticed, bent double and shielding their movement behind the parked vehicles. Reg watched discreetly from a distance as they slipped under each vehicle's chassis, using a cloth here and there to muffle the un-bolting, de-coupling and cable cutting. Finally, they set the precious explosive charges on the vehicles that they could not disable quickly – and sped back to the truck before the lit fuses burnt down.

As the last man leapt aboard, Reg sparked the engine back to life and they headed away at speed. The guard stirred to look around and as he did, the first charges exploded. In seconds, the whole transport base was lit with fires and the alarm sirens began to wail.

'They'll have trouble following us!' joked one of the partisans with satisfaction as Reg headed their truck for the level crossing. Just as the wheels ran onto the tracks, the engine stalled and stopped abruptly, sending the men tumbling over each other in the back.

'*Reggio*, what's going on?' called the commander. *Reggio* turned the engine over again but nothing caught. He closed and opened the choke and tried again. Nothing.

Just then, a train appeared roaring towards them down the track.

'Everyone out and run for it!' called the commander and the men scrambled to the other side of the crossing.

'Leave the truck, Reg!' shouted John, 'Save yourself!'

'Failure is not an option!' said Reg, adding to himself through gritted teeth, 'If I don't get this truck moving, they could all be captured and shot. Focus. Remember what you know!' He heard the train begin to screech its brakes, too close to stop. He pulled out the choke to max, grabbed the wires under the steering wheel to hold them firm and turned the key again. This time, the engine took and Reg slammed on the accelerator, sliding the wheels across the final track and out of danger just as the train thundered past, the tug of its wake dragging the truck sideways across the road.

'*Andiamo!*' called Reg, 'Let's go! Everyone in!' and the partisans leapt back aboard. Reg pushed the engine to its maximum to clear the area, crashing through the gears and the overhanging branches along the lane. They could hear that the first Germans were already in pursuit, having found or stolen some other vehicles, but Reg quickly outpaced them and, with his short cut, lost them in the darkness.

Once back at the farm, the commander helped Reg out of the cab. '*Bravo, Reggio!*' he said, 'That was brave. Stupid, but brave! Well done. You saved the truck – and all our skins!' The other partisans clapped Reg on the back too, each grinning, acknowledgement in their eyes.

John looked at Reg and shook his head. 'Well, if you do become an accountant after the war,' he said, 'you'd better work for the MOD on high risk calculations! Actually, in all seriousness, they have apparently set up a new crack sabotage regiment called the SAS that's as mad and determined as you were tonight!'

'Hmm. Interesting,' said Reg, holding his chin in mock contemplation of the idea, 'I may have a high Mean Average Deviation of craziness, but let's see if I'm quite "M.A.D." enough!' and the two compatriot survivors hugged and grinned.

Paradise

> A mind not to be changed by place or time.
> The mind is its own place, and in itself
> Can make a heav'n of hell, a hell of heav'n.
> John Milton, *Paradise Lost*

Despite all the secrecy, somehow the story of Reg's daring success spread. The Chiesa family had a hero in their midst – a man whose determination beat the odds, saved the truck and brought all the fighters safely home.

The next evening, Domenico and Marina arranged a special meal to celebrate and some of the partisans joined them before the curfew. The food was simple but good. Reg was allowed to help Maria and Marina in making the polenta and sauce. Being able to stand close to Maria and see the admiration in her eyes was reward enough for his exploits. She sat next to him for the meal too, where she would normally sit between her mother and one of her brothers. This was another sign that her growing affection for him had been accepted by the family.

There was plenty of joking and laughter during the meal, then, to everyone's delight, Domenico again got out his *fisarmonica*. The partisans started the singing with their romantic revolutionary song, *Bella Ciao*. The lyrics sing of a partisan who fights for freedom and knows he may die. He asks to be buried in the mountains under a beautiful flower, so that passers-by will admire the flower and say it is the flower of the partisan who died for freedom!

Reg listened intently to the song, singing along to the repeated refrain in each verse, '*O Bella, ciao, Bella, ciao! Bella, ciao, ciao, ciao!*' (Goodbye, my beautiful!). As the song ended he whispered to Maria, 'There is only one beautiful flower for me and she is right here!' Maria blushed and giggled.

As dusk approached the partisans started to take their leave. The sky was already streaked with the first pink blushes of the descending sun. There would be a beautiful sunset from the hilltops. Reg darted over to one of the partisans, Marco, who was about to leave on his small motorbike, 'May I borrow this, just for tonight, please?' Marco looked back over Reg's shoulder towards the house and saw Maria, pretending not to watch them. '*Certo, Reggio!*' of course! Marco said with a wink. He got off the motorbike and ran over to a comrade to double up for a lift home. They waved as they left.

Signor Domenico walked over, puzzled. Reg turned to him and stood to attention. In his best Italian, he politely requested permission to show Maria the sunset. Domenico frowned a little, his thick moustache twitching in the way that it did when he was considering something. He shot a look at his daughter, whose large brown eyes were pleading with him. '*Bene, bene,*' (alright then), he said. '*Grazie mille!*' (A thousand thank yous!) said Reg with a small bow. Maria ran forward. '*Grazie, Papà!*' (Thank you Papa!)

She carefully mounted the motorbike behind Reg, keeping her skirts well out of the way of the wheels. Reg started the engine and revved it a little to gauge its power. '*Tieni forte!*' (Hold on tight!) Tentatively, she slipped her arms around his chest to hold on and, as smoothly as he could, Reg moved off with his precious passenger.

The light breeze blew through her hair and the low slung sun splashed the couple with dappled patches of gold. They rode under the trees, up and up to the top – to the best view. Reg knew just the right place to stop from his earlier excursions with the partisans, even though those trips were mainly in the dark. The view across the landscape in daylight was stupendous, and now the sunset colours bathed the valley in a glorious, warm glow.

Maria gasped, '*Molto bello!*' (Very beautiful!)

Reg could not have wished for a better opportunity to compliment this lovely young woman. All he needed to do was to change the masculine *bello* to the feminine *bella*. '*Molto bella, dico io!*' (I say, beautiful you!) Maria looked up at him and laughed shyly. He gently cupped her lovely face in his hands and kissed her warm, rosy lips.

Too soon, the pinks and golds had darkened to reds and mauves as the shadows lengthened and the curfew was almost due. Reg helped Maria onto the motorbike and rode with the utmost care back to the farmhouse. Domenico was waiting. They were just in time. The bike was moved out of sight for the night and the young couple slipped indoors. Domenico bolted the stout old door firmly after them, sealing out the darkening night.

10

Rastrellamento! – Hunt Down and Round Up

So disasters come not singly;
But as if they watched and waited,
Scanning one another's motions.
When the first descends the others
Follow, follow, gathering flock-wise,
Round their victim, sick and wounded,
First a shadow, then a sorrow,
Till the air is dark with anguish.

Henry Wadsworth Longfellow, *The Song of Hiawatha*

The raid was successful. The operating capacity of a major local Nazi base was destroyed, at least for the time being. But this deadly game of cat-and-mouse with the occupying force had consequences for the civilians too. The pressure on the population to pass any information to the Nazis about who was involved increased. Somewhere in the mesh of war, the occupiers believed, there are always loose threads. It takes a pull on just one strand to unravel the whole. After just a few days, the search for the lose threads began.

Shortly after midnight there was an urgent, repeated knocking at the door of the Chiesa household. Domenico hurried down, struggling to wake up as he pulled back the bolts. He opened it to see one of the young *partigiani* outside. '*Rastrellamento!*' House raid in the village! The young man whispered urgently in an anxious tone and ran on to the next house that harboured an illicit Allied soldier. The Germans were combing the area for Allied forces being concealed by peasant families.

Quickly, the door was re-bolted. By the light of just one candle, Signor Chiesa woke Reg who scrambled with his pillow into the prearranged hiding place while his bedding was rolled quickly and placed in a cupboard, as if normally stored there. It was still warm. Would the searchers feel it? The fearful father quickly ran a check through his mind. Could everything Reg had in the house, or had used here, be explained? His male clothes? His female clothes? Did he have anything else? He hurried back to the second wine cellar to ask. Reg reassured him. He was always ready. He had not just taken his pillow with him for comfort! His Bible, dictionary and his notes were kept inside. As long as they did not find him and his pillow, there would be no trace of him in the house that could not be explained. The anxious father breathed a sigh of relief. He snuffed out the candle, went back to lie on his bed and wait.

Soon, fists were hammering on the front door and the harsh voice of a soldier in Nazi military uniform demanded entry. Domenico opened the door without a word and six soldiers marched in with their helmets, heavy boots and weapons at the ready. They strode into every room, opening cupboards and throwing clothes and belongings onto the floor as they checked for hidden enemies. They marched into the yard and pulled open the chicken coup, bayoneted the wood store and toppled the stack of grain sacks so that they tumbled down. They watched the bags fall for signs of a heavier sack, perhaps holding a hidden body. They knew the tricks by now. With the hens clucking and dogs barking, they checked the pig sty, adding to the tense chaos of the night with squeals of indignation from its small, new occupant.

Back inside the house, they clambered up into the eaves and finally demanded to go into the cellar. The father cautiously opened the trap door to the main cellar in the kitchen floor and two soldiers pushed him aside and went down. Silence. The soldiers had learnt to wait and listen for the sound of breathing. They heard and saw nothing. Annoyed, one of the men, pointing at the rows of slightly dusty bottles, said in German what sounded like, 'Shouldn't we at least take something back for the captain?' They re-emerged each clutching a couple of bottles of wine.

The family kept their eyes firmly fixed on their feet, desperate not to look at the rug and give away the secret, second cellar. The patrol captain took a look at the good, strong colour of the wine, smiled to approve the trophy then signalled to the door and the men marched out. As he left, the captain cast a last look around the room. He barked a warning at Signor Chiesa, 'We'll be back,' and closed the door with a thud behind him.

Slowly, the sons and daughter, wife and husband, gathered in their nightclothes to stare together at the closed door. Signor Chiesa put his arm round his wife and the three grown children drew close to hold each other in trembling silence.

When would they come back? Tonight? Where would they go now? Would they find someone in another house? No one could rest and it was still too early to think that the raid was over.

At last, Marina stoked the glowing embers in the stove to boil some water for hot lemon tea. Reg must stay hidden, at least until the morning. She had just placed a tray with five steaming glasses on the table for the family to share, when the sound of gunfire was heard. She jumped and let out a small cry, then stood still, tingling with fear, the hair on her arms raised. Everyone strained to listen. How many shots? How many victims? A new and deeper silence seemed to mat the threads of darkness tighter around them and strangle the very breath from the night.

No one went to bed. Sleep was impossible, so they gradually tidied the mess of scattered belongings that the soldiers had left, then dozed in a chair or looked out of the window at a lifeless sky. But by the first light of dawn, Marina realised that the pattern of the day had to appear normal. They must not show that they knew something terrible had happened in the night, and why. They must feign innocence to save the innocent. The family dressed for the new morning and each began the daily chores. At last, Guido collected Reg from the secret extra cellar space, but asked him to stay out of sight, upstairs and away from any windows, while they waited to hear the news. There was no hurry. It was going to be bad.

At around lunchtime, a neighbour came over with some milk in a churn, as an excuse to call. Yes, the *partigiani* had heard rumours that there was an informant, but this was rare and no one was identified, so it could have been a random check, like so many before. The Nazis spread the gossip too that they were tipped off, but they often said that in order to sow doubt and division among the villagers. The raid might have been a reprisal for the burning of their vehicles. Whatever the reason, they decided to scour the village and look for escapees – and, this time, they found one.

The patrols knew to check the outbuildings and stores as well as the houses. For heating and cooking purposes, the Italian peasant farmers used brushwood, which was stored outside, piled roof-high. Whenever Italian Fascists or enemy troops were spotted in the vicinity, it was necessary for the *évadés* (the French word for escapees was often used by the Allies) to get underneath or behind this extensive pile of brushwood. If he was caught, not only would he be executed because he was not in uniform, but the threat was always made that so too would the entire family harbouring him, including the children.

This time, the target was a fellow British escapee. He had been suffering from the flu and was laid up in a barn. Whether or not someone noticed something and reported it was unclear. The soldiers searched the barn and found him. They dragged him into the yard and shot him dead. It was as yet unclear if the host family had shared the same fate.

Mother Marina let out a cry and clapped her hand to her mouth. Her knees gave way and her husband stepped forward to take her in his arms and stop her falling, even as his own eyes filled with tears of sorrow and fury. Their sons and daughter approached softly and encircled the grieving couple. The neighbour mumbled his own condolences and slipped away with his churn to visit the next house.

Reg had crept out onto the top of the open wooden staircase, hidden from view, to listen. As he heard the words, he put an arm against the wall to steady himself and sat down heavily on one stair, staring at the wall in disbelief, repeating the Italian words to himself to check what he had heard and if he had really understood it right. *Ucciso*, shot. *Morto*, dead. He leant forward to look down at his own protectors through the rails and his blood ran cold at the thought that his fellow internee and escapee had paid the ultimate price in this war. He thought of the family back in England and how they would be shattered by the news, when it finally reached them. Then his mind wandered to his own family. The searchers could have found him too – and his fate would have been the same! But it was not only that. He was a soldier after all, and death was always a possible outcome of that role. Worse still, his wonderful Chiesa family could have been killed just as easily. He could have caused their deaths – even the death of his lovely Maria. The true meaning of the handshake he had shared with the head of the partisans on the night of his arrival in this family, the harsh reality of the responsibility and the risk, struck home. The thought burnt in his head, branded there, like a shocking image that, once seen, remains forever imprinted on the inner eye.

That evening, a cold supper was served in silence. The songs and jokes of other evenings seemed far distant from the fear and sorrow that had now flooded their home. The World War had invaded their small village again, bringing wanton destruction and desperate, cruel sadness.

Reg looked from face to face around the table. All eyes were cast down, the family members adrift in their own thoughts. The father's ready smile had retreated beneath his fine moustache and a deep frown ploughed furrows between the dark brows. The two grown sons still ate hungrily, but their usual competitive energy and humorous banter was stilled, weighted by grief and fear. The mother barely touched her food. A stifled sob shook her shoulders from time to time and an involuntary tear followed another down her cheek and onto the plate.

Maria, pale and with slightly shaking hand, patted her mother's arm to comfort her. Reg could not help but be startled again by her beauty, even now, with her radiant skin, pale from tiredness, contrasted against her rich dark wavy hair that flowed smoothly past her cheek, down her neck and over her shoulders. As she looked up and caught his gaze, the tears brimming in her dark eyes glinted in the low light and seemed to flash, taking his breath away. But even as every fibre of his being cried out to touch her, to hold her close and to tell her that he would make it alright, he knew that this tragedy signalled a change beyond his control, that the time had come for separation.

As the hours ticked by that night, he lay on the straw bed unable to rest. His heart broke for his compatriot's relatives back home, for the brave host family and all the other poor families whose peace had been invaded by fear that night. His chest tightened at the very thought of leaving Maria – yet leave he knew he must. There would be another raid, and possibly quite soon, so for him to stay longer in their home was too risky for everyone. He shuddered again at the thought of being responsible for any harm to the Chiesa family. No, he must go and make sure all trace of his presence there was erased.

The war had already wrung from this young man, barely more than a schoolboy at his enrolment, more deep emotions than he thought possible. He had felt intense fear, rage beyond words, a drive to survive, the inhuman, bestial malice needed to push aside a lifetime of Christian indoctrination and to shoot to kill another man. He had found that men he took to be the 'enemy' in the Italian leaders of the camp, could act as friends. He had shared life-threatening experiences with people in the partisans whose political ideals he did not believe in. He had built bonds of comradeship that only death could break and had willingly faced dangers that the bright-eyed young grammar school boy could never have imagined.

Yet the man he had become was frightened. He was about to step outside the warm, comforting embrace of this rural community that had shielded him for many months from the harshest realities of the war outside. He had been welcomed, fed, taught new skills and cocooned. Domenico had entrusted to him the safety of his home, his livelihood, his very life and the lives of his wife, his sons and daughter. He had even tolerated *Reggio's* conquest of the heart of his darling daughter, Maria, and had recently even accepted the possibility that their clear attraction and affection for each other might lead to a permanent union, one day.

Now, abruptly, *Reggio* was going to have to step away and not look back. Any contact with the family after he had left would put them in danger again – from the Nazis, from the Italian Fascists and who knows what other vengeances. It could be years before they were able to meet again and by then what else may have come between them? Would he survive? Would they survive? Would Maria remember him or would another handsome beau whisk her away to a new life once this hell was over and done? He was caught in a tangle of love, fear, anger, violence and hatred not of his making – war.

He wanted to cry, or howl or shout. Instead he clenched his fists, tears trying and failing to squeeze from his eyes, watching, waiting for the inevitable arrival of the next dawn.

11

Escape

Every one of us is born, and everyone dies.
However, three of every ten seem to be born to live,
Three seem to be born to die, and three live lifefully or deathfully
according to their chosen life styles.
But only one in ten seems to survive all dangers…

Lao Tzu, *Tao Te Ching, Verse 50, The Forces of Life and Death*

The following morning, as soon as it was light, the leader of the partisans arrived with one of his men. Both were armed. 'We are moving all the remaining escapees to new hosts or sending them away. There will be another search – and soon – and we can't expect our host families to face any unnecessary risks. It's time for the Allied military to leave now.'

The menfolk gathered to greet the visitors, abandoning the morning chores that they had sleepily begun. Marina and Maria joined them from the kitchen, Maria with a blanket around her shoulders against the early morning chill.

'What will happen to them?' she asked.

'We'll offer them the chance to go and reach their troops in the south or escape to another country. More than that we can't share. This village is no longer safe for them or for us while they are here.'

Within a few minutes, Reg had collected his dictionary, his notes and dressed in the clothes he wore for night excursions with the partisans, ready to leave. He had spent the night thinking about what he could possibly say to his hosts, how he could possibly thank them. After hours of staring at the ceiling, rejecting speech after speech, he realised that he should simply say a heartfelt 'thank you', show them that he remembered the happy moments they had shared and tell them that he would never forget their kindness.

He joined the family, who had gathered by the front door. The father, Domenico, tapped the small dictionary. 'You don't need that now!' He joked, 'You have learnt well! *Reggio*, you are almost an Italian!' He slapped Reg on the back. Reg turned and hugged him, then it was the turn of the two brothers, Guido and Gianni. He thanked each for tolerating his jokes and for putting up with his amateur work in the fields. Each responded with a warm hug.

'I must of course take every visible trace of myself with me,' he said solemnly. Then with a little twinkle in his eye, he took the mother Marina's hand and kissed it gallantly, 'but I leave with you the memories of our songs together and my gratitude to you forever in this place of yours that you have made my home.' Quickly turning to Maria and taking her hand in both of his, he continued as if speaking to the whole family, but staring directly into the chestnut warmth of her tear-filled eyes added, 'And in this wonderful home, I leave you my heart!'

⌒ — ⌒

A few miles away down a narrow side street, in the house of the quietly spoken and bespectacled leader of the partisans, preparations for the safe departure of the POWs were already in full swing. Reg and John returned to the house they had first entered after their days and nights on the run from the camp, taken there by the vine-grower and his son.

The escapees were assembled and assessed to decide who might pass for Italian. Simple hair dye could turn many a blond Brit into a passable Italian – as long as they did not speak. These POWs were sent off to be photographed in a neighbouring house, ready for the preparation of false identity and travel documents. Reg fitted into this category. His knowledge of the language would be an added advantage. He would probably understand most of what was going on around him and be able to react appropriately, in gestures at least, even if it was better to avoid speaking with his still rather too obvious English accent. The partisans could use his language skill in planning his escape, to make him appear more Italian and so increase his chances of success.

Il Capo dei Partigiani, the leader of the partisans was leaning over the large kitchen table at which they had drunk wine on that first night in the village. It was now spread with maps of rail lines and roads so that the routes could be planned – routes that this time, and with the support of these brave freedom fighters, would help them to make it out alive. The aim was to avoid overlapping the paths of too many escapees at once. Routes had to be changed frequently, as soon as it was suspected that they were being observed, so a variety of alternative plans were followed to keep the enemy guessing. Each escapee had to memorise the details of their particular route, so that as little as possible was written down. Code-named counterparts in other areas along the way were being contacted through safe channels with instructions of when and where to guide the POWs at each junction point on their journey. Physical signs and signals were put in place that would seem like a natural part of everyday life, but which would be a life-saving connection for each man – a particular hat, the offer of a cigarette, the conventions of a church service. Reg marvelled at the organisation and preparedness. This seemed like a national underground network of local volunteers that must have been painstakingly built over the months and years – and at great risk to each and every member.

Since Reg was one of those who could pass for Italian, it was decided he should attempt one of the escape routes north to Switzerland. He was given a replacement set of clothes and a workman's cap and told that the only possession he could take was his Italian dictionary – and that had to be well hidden. Against the rules and in fact quite foolishly, he concealed some of his notes carefully. He wanted to be able to ask for compensation for those who had helped him, but knew he had to be ready to destroy these scraps of paper at any time. His tough army boots sadly had to be left behind, replaced with some cheap but typical workman's shoes.

The instructions are clear. Each man has to follow his own route and, once on his way, cannot acknowledge another escapee at any point. If he does, that will put everyone involved in danger. Survival depends on strict discipline and staying alert to avoid mistakes at all times. The POWs hug each other and wish each other luck. Tears glisten in Reg's blue eyes as he and John say goodbye. The bond formed by their shared experiences will not be broken, even if they are never to meet again. They shake the hands of the *partigiani* or hug them too. They owe these people their lives and know only too well that the partisans and their families will remain in danger long after the journeys of this group of Allied men are over.

All too soon, it is time to go.

On St George's Day, 23 April, 1944, Reg is given a train ticket and a matchbox and is taken to the railway station at Felegara-Sant'Andrea Bagni. His pulse starts racing as the reality of the situation strikes home. He is back on the run, as he had been with John. He will either get to Switzerland and live, or the next few days could be his last.

He glances casually along the platform and spots two other escapees from the group – two majors – who are waiting for the same train. They must all look out for a woman in a red beret arriving to join the train. Finally, just as the train draws into the station, a lady in a smart, dark-coloured wool jacket and skirt, and wearing a bright red beret, set off by a red flower brooch on the revere collar of the jacket, walks onto the platform. She chooses a carriage and steps inside. As instructed, Reg boards but sits a few carriages behind her. 'Remember to look relaxed, as if you travel on this train regularly,' he reminds himself, but it is hard to sit still, knowing he has to check at every station to see if she gets off or not and to follow her if she does. He decides to stand nonchalantly by the window, toying with a cigarette, as if thinking of smoking it but remaining undecided. He only has two cigarettes for the whole journey, so he has to make this one last as long as possible.

At Fidenza, the red beret leaves the train and Reg slips out to follow her, remaining a cautious few metres away. The woman in the red beret crosses the platform to catch the express bound for Milan and her casual observers follow suit. The platform is not too busy, which is both good and bad. There are fewer people to see them, but not enough people to hide them in a crowd. 'Milan will be different, probably better,' he reassures himself and settles in to watch the countryside rush past, only too glad that he is not having to cross it on foot.

As they draw into Milan station, Reg is horrified to see that the platform is milling with high-ranking German officers and their batmen handling the suitcases and equipment. '*Reggio*, keep a cool head. Remember, you are an Italian,' he tells himself. 'Keep your eyes on the red beret. You are a worker with no reason to engage with any of these men.' He adopts the part he has to play, feeling glad that he has worked in the fields and seen the gait and mannerisms of the farming peasants. He consciously relaxes his shoulders and changes his walk. Behind the act, it is intriguing and surreal to pass between these enemy uniforms, surrounded by the clipped sounds of the language of the occupiers and yet appear to be invisible to them. Separately, he and the two British majors make their way out to the street.

The red beret bobs amongst the crowds and over to the bus station, where the wearer stops to speak to a man who is waiting for a particular bus. This is the transfer signal. Now Reg is to wait at the bus stop behind the man, while the red beret takes a new direction away, her task completed.

There are some German soldiers standing around waiting too. After a moment or two, the new contact man takes out a cigarette and flips it skilfully into his pursed lips. He pats his pockets, clearly looking for matches that are not there.

He turns and asks Reg for a light, which Reg understands and, without replying, hands over the matchbox he was given. The man lights the cigarette and takes a puff gratefully, then deftly passes Reg a ticket for the bus as he returns the matchbox to him. Soon, the bus arrives and Reg carefully hangs back to avoid drawing attention to his connection with the contact. He finds a pair of empty seats and sits by the window. A moment later, one of the German soldiers takes the place next to him. Reg keeps his eyes on the window to avoid making eye contact or prompting any comment from the new passenger. How could he avoid that for the whole journey, though? 'Think, *Reggio!* You are *Italiano*,' he tells himself again. 'You are a tired worker travelling reluctantly to the end of the line, so what would you do on a bus? Of course – you would take a nap.' Reg pulls the cap forward over his eyes, slides down in the seat with his arms folded and pretends to sleep, slumped against the dusty glass of the window.

When the bus arrives at the bus terminus, Reg waits for the rest of the passengers to disembark, pretending to rouse himself from his slumbers with difficulty. He sees the contact leave the bus and heads off in the same direction, but walking on the other side of the street. The man goes into a church, where a service is in progress. He enters and finds a pew to sit down. Reg follows, sitting at the back and keeping his head bowed, pretending to pray.

At a given point in the service, the usher moves from pew to pew with the collection plate, but Reg has no coins, no money at all to put in it. He hears the Bible story of the widow giving to the church her last mite echoing in his ears and a feels a cold sweat on his brow as the usher approaches. How will the usher react if he puts nothing at all in the plate? Reg hopes the partisans have thought about this situation already and decides to show his empty hands, '*Mi dispiace…*' (I'm sorry…) he whispers. The usher nods knowingly and presses Reg's shoulder down gently but firmly, as if to say, 'Wait here!'

At the end of the service, when everyone else has left, Reg stays, head down as if still deep in prayer. The usher returns and signals to Reg with a tap on the shoulder and a nod, that he should follow behind. In a side chapel, a man is waiting. The usher bows and leaves. The man turns and smiles. He shakes Reg by the hand. 'I am your guide, Umbertino Granata,' he says. 'Come with me!' The guide leads Reg to a flat where he must wait till the evening. 'Where are we going to cross?' asks Reg. 'It's best if you don't know the exact details. You have seen that we are not far from Como Chiasso, but that's as much as I can tell you. We have to go to the border from here on foot,' explains the guide. 'It is not an easy route, so get some rest now.'

After dark, Umbertino returns. 'Did you get some sleep?' he asks.

'A little,' comes Reg's unconvincing reply. It is impossible to relax with the border so near and the risks so high.

'Stay close but walk naturally next to me, as if we are friends, co-workers finishing a shift and so out after the curfew. Say nothing till we are past the last house,' warns the guide.

They set off together silently. After a while, the path ends and they climb a low fence to start crossing open country. There are empty fields, thickets to push through and streams to cross. The dark outlines of cattle dot the landscape and they weave past farmhouses, outhouses, barns and huts, closer and closer to the Swiss border.

By the middle of the night, they reach a high wire fence that blocks the path. The guide explains that it is guarded by patrols who walk a mile in each direction and back again. This is the border. This is the last and perhaps most dangerous part. Anyone seen out at night here will be shot on sight. Umbertino points across the land in front of them and explains the next steps. 'There is a brief window of time when you can get past the guards, through the fence and out of range on the other side before the guard returns.'

'How do I get past the fence?'

'There are water culverts under the fence at intervals of a quarter of a mile. This one, straight ahead, is the one you must go through. You climb into the culvert and up through the pipe. You then run straight on to the river, swim across it and climb up the bank on the other side. Then you are in Switzerland.'

Reg nods, taking it all in and repeating it in his mind, as if to draw a sketched map of the words, so as not to miss a detail.

'Good luck!' whispers his guide. 'I will give you the signal when to move.'

'*Grazie!* Thank you for everything!' says Reg, gripping the guide's hand in a firm and heartfelt gesture of gratitude.

It is a tense wait. Reg can feel his heart thumping louder and faster in his chest. He closes his eyes and breathes in slowly. 'Stay calm,' he tells himself. 'Save your strength.' When the guards next march away, the guide nods and nudges Reg gently on the back, his signal to go. Reg runs forward and scrambles through the culvert. The cold water is trickling down as he tries to climb up. He slips and slides through the constantly flowing film of water and strands of slime, but pushes forward, up and out. Glancing right and left, he listens for the rush of the river. There! Straight ahead. He runs across the open strip of land to the river, keeping his head low. He looks anxiously from side to side as he runs. In the dark he can make out what seems to be a small town or village with a bridge over the river to the right. How easy it would be in peacetime to walk across it! But not now and not tonight. It is just a few metres more to the river, though it feels so much further. Reaching the bank, he knows he must not hesitate. Each second counts. So he slides his body quickly over the grassy edge and into the swift current. The water is freezing cold – fed by the mountain streams – and he has to suppress the instant urge to gasp out loud as he struggles to control his shivers. He pulls his fully clothed body through the fast-moving waters and makes headway to get across to the other bank before the patrolling guards turn back towards him.

The spring flow is strong and he cannot cross straight but has to work with the water to cut a diagonal line across. In the darkness, he must keep the goal clear in his sights – the black outline of the bushes on the far bank. He hauls each arm out of the swirling, dragging water, weighed down with the simple jacket, and again and again plunges each one back in to pull himself nearer to the vague silhouette ahead. He heaves at his muscles that are weak with cold, his teeth starting to chatter involuntarily. 'Not now! You can't fail now!' he says to himself.

As if on cue, an image from his training days enters his mind. He suddenly remembers – and he smiles even in that desperate moment of *extremis* – the shouting face of the sergeant major and his seeming relish at making the young recruits march into the icy Welsh sea. That apparently pointless activity now makes perfect sense. This river crossing in the dark and cold is exactly the kind of test that his training was preparing him to face. Still smiling, and despite the icy water rushing all round him, he feels a warm surge of gratitude run through his body. Another image flickers into his mind: of his photo in his officer's uniform and regimental cap, decorated with its symbolic badge of a deer, a hart, fording a river. 'This is my ford and I am a Hertfordshire lad!' he tells himself, gritting his teeth and willing his arms and legs forward through the icy flow. The thought of Hertfordshire, of home, of support and a place where he belongs strengthens his determination. He pushes ahead with new energy for the last few strokes until, at last, he can grasp hold of the tough, wild grasses on the opposite bank.

He hauls himself up out of the water, dripping wet and with the soles of the cheap shoes flapping. There is no time to catch his breath – and he will surely succumb to the cold if he stops now. Reg casts a glance around then heads up the slope away from the river as fast as he can. He is keen to get to the cover of some trees perhaps a few dozen yards up the slope. He must be out of sight before a returning guard has a chance to spot his shadowy figure against the hillside.

As a country boy, he knows that you catch the rabbit when it moves, not when it is still, but move he must. The huntsman here is his enemy, like the sniper in the dark that took Private Wells's life just inches from him on that dark North African night. 'I will get through! I will!'

He trips in his broken shoes, falls, picks himself up, sets off again. He is crouching as low as possible, bitterly cold, soaking wet, trying not to lose his footing again in the scrubby undergrowth. All his thoughts are of the danger behind him, of the patrolling guard with his rifle perhaps aiming right now at his back. With a lurch he reaches the tree line and gratefully stumbles a few paces into the cover of the trees.

Suddenly in the dark, he hears the click of a gun being cocked a few metres ahead. He stops still in shock and fear, not daring to look up in its direction. Then he hears the challenge barked out in German, '*Hände hoch!*' (Put your hands up!)

He stands immobile in the pose of running, dumbfounded and shivering with cold and disbelief. No! No! Fear takes hold – a gun is pointed directly at him. Is this how it ends? But then fear is quickly replaced by a strange feeling of guilt. After all the seven and a half months of effort by so many to hide him and keep him safe, has he really fallen back into the hands of the Germans somehow? This should be the Italian part of Switzerland, so why is a German here? Confused and unwilling to accept being taken prisoner a second time, he puts his hands in the air and walks slowly forward, head bowed. 'There's always a way out. There has to be!' he thinks and glances furtively to the side to try to spot an opportunity to dart behind some larger trees and escape recapture. The guard stands pointing his gun at the dripping and bedraggled figure, but it is not aimed and ready to fire. Instead, he is resting it nonchalantly on one hip, so that he can casually light a cigarette with his free hand. At the sound of the striking match, Reg looks up at the figure in the feeble glow of the flame – and sees that the guard's uniform is Swiss! Relief like a hot wave floods through his whole being. He collapses onto his knees in the scrub.

The guard is Swiss-German. He is safe.

12

Sacrifices Unknown

Over all our happy country,
Over all our Nation spread,
Is our band of noble heroes,
Is our army of the dead.

Will Carleton, *Farm Ballads,* 1873.

Back in the Italian hotel that evening, Beth reread the final pages of her grandfather's notes before laying them back in the suitcase,

So on 24th April 1944, just seven and a half months after getting out of the prisoner-of-war camp, I arrived in Switzerland. I still had my Italian grammar and dictionary, soaked and damaged as it was on that occasion.

After delousing and with a change of civilian clothes, I was taken to the Headquarters of the British Troops in the Canton of St Gallen, at Wil. I gave them my report and was thoroughly interrogated about my time in Italy. New duties kept me in Switzerland until I was finally released and able to inform my family that I was coming home shortly before Christmas, 1944.

'So that is how he survived. That's how I came to be here. Yes, he had strength, determination, courage beyond words at such a young age, but most of all he had the help of so many people who were just as strong, smart, determined and brave – and who were ready to sacrifice everything including themselves and their loved ones to save others – to save my Dadu.'

Suddenly, she felt ashamed that she had not thought of it before, thought how there were so many Dadus and so many people who had done and given so much. The expressions of gratitude were repeated every year on 11 November,

Remembrance Day, but this act of gratitude and remembrance had never felt so true, so raw. 'We must lay flowers at their graves,' she said.

'Where?' asked Robert.

'For all of them, I suppose!' she said, 'Let's go to the village cemetery tomorrow.'

Robert had suggested that they hire bikes this time, so that they could feel closer to the natural environment. Beth thought this was a lovely idea and agreed, forgetting that the taxi they had taken before had driven almost vertically upwards for several miles! Robert found a bike hire outlet but, since it was summer, they were all out on loan. The only vehicle they had left was a tandem. 'That's alright!' said Robert, trying to make the best of it, 'We'll manage!' Beth looked doubtful. She remembered his tales of disaster and regretted having agreed to this idea. But here they were, so she would go along with it on one condition. And the condition was this: 'Only if I'm at the front,' she said firmly.

The sun was already high, bright and hot by the time they were ready to leave. They set out with a basket on the front handlebars full of flowers, safely in jars of water, for the graves. They suddenly felt excited about returning to the village where they had found such warmth and dedication. This burst of energy turned out to be essential – but though they panted up most of the steep road, they finally had to give up to walk the last stretch. Beth was about to complain about the ridiculous idea of taking a tandem for such a hilly ride when a car full of villagers revved past, engine straining with the climb.

The window was wound down and an arm gestured out of it. *'Forza! Forza!'* (More power! More power!) came the encouragement, accompanied by peals of laughter from the other passengers as they crawled past the sweating riders. Robert gave a weak smile and a limp wave. Beth, hot, thirsty and battling to keep the tandem handlebars straight and climb this steep slope at the same time, was about to get cross. Then she recognised one of the genuinely cheerful faces in the car as someone from the café and accepted the playful intention in their high spirits. She smiled back, a broad happy smile. There certainly was a life-force here, an energy mixed with appreciation for the effort these foreigners were making to connect with the rugged landscape, and – like Reg himself and the villagers too – not to be beaten by it.

The rich greens and golds of the bushes competing for space at the roadside, the tumbling flowers on the climbers that scrambled up the trees, the dancing butterflies that seemed to accompany their rise into the hills – all set a wonderful atmosphere of calm amongst the richness of nature. Beth and Robert passed the 600-metre altitude sign and shortly afterwards rounded the top of the next crest. Though still upwards, the gentler slope was a welcome respite from the climb, and led them on towards the village. Then they turned down a lane and cycled on towards the cemetery. They found it nestled in amongst the trees as if gently protected by their sheltering branches. Inside the boundary wall, over which tumbled the blooms of red bougainvilleas, stood rows of family vaults. The white marble front panels enclosing each commemorative vault were dappled with shade as the sun filtered through the surrounding trees.

Beth felt her heart beat faster. Was she about to find evidence of betrayal and murder? Would she find news of post-war lives in peace and happiness? At first, she moved slowly and reverently along the marble shelves of small cupboard-like tombs. Then gradually she found herself walking more quickly, as she scanned the lettering for names from Reg's list of hosts. Each panel displayed the photograph and name of each member of the family, along with the dates of their lives. Where were they? They must be here! Then she saw it – Domenico Chiesa – and Marina Chiesa was next to him! She stopped, and took an involuntary deep breath to steady herself. 'Look!' she called out, and glanced across to Robert who hurried over. The faces of an elderly couple smiled out from oval frames on the two white marble plaques, side by side. Below these calming images, the simple dates of their passing confirmed that they had lived long lives. She let out a laugh of relief, and spontaneously hugged Robert. The Chiesas' secret had remained safe! Gratefully, she added flowers to the waiting wall-vases by each name. Robert and Beth stood together for a moment in silence. The petals of the flowers fanned gently in the light breeze and reminded her that this journey had begun amidst the floral tributes at her grandfather's funeral. She sighed again and whispered, 'Thank you!' then calmly moved on to look for the next name on the list, and the next.

⌇ — ⌇

A few months later, on a chilly 11 November that year, Beth and Robert stood in the street together to witness the annual national memorial service at the Cenotaph in London, each with a new understanding of the true, deep meaning that the immense and solemn ceremony held. When they returned to her London flat afterwards for coffee, Beth unpinned the red poppy from her coat and laid it on the side table.

'My mother always says that once the duties of Poppy Day are done, we can start to think about Christmas,' said Robert, sinking into a chair.

'Christmas!' exclaimed Beth. 'Of course, why didn't I think of that before?'

'What do you mean?'

'He finally got home at Christmas time. After the hiding, the escape, the debrief in Switzerland, he was only finally allowed back by Christmas. Until he was permitted to contact them, the family wouldn't have known if he was alive or dead!' she exclaimed, startled by this new thought.

'Of course, yes. How awful for them to live with the uncertainty for all that time,' said Robert.

'Just imagine!' she responded, now deep in thought, 'And how must it have felt that first Christmas back home?'

Beth went to stand by the window and looked out as the first lazy flakes of light snow tried unsuccessfully to fall through the chill, grey air. She looked up at the gloomy sky and strained to imagine the final scenes that closed such a huge chapter for her grandfather and opened the path for the rest of his life – the many decades of life that followed from the sacrifices which so many people had made for him. She began to understand that his life – and in turn her life was only possible thanks to the courage and generosity of those Italian people. At last she understood why he chose their music, the music and song of their beautiful country, to send him on his final journey. It was there, in Italy, that his life was saved, with their songs held deep inside him. And it was they, those brave Italians, who had guided him to safety.

She picked up the newly framed double photo on the windowsill. Her great-grandfather, Edward and her grandfather Reginald Edward, at the same age, heroes in different ways in two different wars. No wonder they had spoken so little about their lives in the war. How could anyone else understand? Only those who were there would know the extremes of emotion, the depth of feeling, the strain of being pushed to the limits, physically, emotionally, morally, psychologically. She felt so grateful that she had been the one to trace their story and to learn about these lives that had led to hers. She felt connected so closely now with this past that she knew it would change the way she thought about her future. How lucky she had been to be able to discover the story through his papers, letters and maps, but also through visits to the sites and scenes of that story. Because of his struggles and those of so many countless others through those terrible years she, on her journey, had been able to enjoy peaceful travels, excellent country wine and wonderful good company – safe and happy in the warmth of the Italian sun.

She looked at the faces of father and son and her brow furrowed. How had it felt when they met again? The elder soldier with his experience of horrifying trench warfare, unimaginable loss, and the guilt of survival. The younger officer returning from conflict with his own dreadful experiences and a new under-standing of his father. She thought of the Round House Lodge, of the old village of Ware and the exceptionally cold winter that befell northern Europe in 1944. She started to build a picture in her mind of how it might have been.

'What do you think? Could it have been like this, Robert?'

13

The Return

To be loved is the greatest honour of all.
Anon.

The autumn of 1944 is a golden autumn. In the warm evenings after his work in the garden of the big house, Edward brings in the last of the summer crop from his own vegetable patch, and plants some winter cabbages for his family. Victor tries to be a good son and brother, but he always feels there is a space he cannot fill. Reg had been so perfect – clever, hard-working, determined and striking with his bright blue eyes and athletic build. No, he must not talk in the past tense. His brother will be back. He has to be!

Armistice Day comes on the eleventh of November, as it has every year since 1919, after that first terrible war. But no news arrives. Their father packs Reg's best Sunday boots in a box and takes all reminders of him to the bedroom where he slept before he left. The old soldier never says a word, but spends hours in the room and his daughter Kathleen thinks she sometimes hears him cry.

As the autumn of 1944 cools to frosty days and icy nights, Kathleen and Victor cannot help but wonder if their brother is somewhere in Europe, cold, hungry, trying to battle his way home – and if anyone is helping him. They have agreed always to imagine him alive, because not to do so would be a pain impossible to bear.

When Christmas approaches, they prepare for another year without Reg. They hang decorations and save ration tokens to manage the extra demands of making the festive dishes. Christmas puddings with most, if not all of the usual ingredients have been steamed and lie in their glass bowls, tied in cloth. They have been resting in the cool air of an unheated bedroom, under mother's bed, since the middle of October, for the full flavours of the brandy to soak into the dried fruit and suet.

The family work through the traditions of Advent, keeping up appearances, like the other townsfolk. At the carol service in mid-December, just the centre pews of the small village church are open. The pastor says that closing off the side transepts is to save heat and candles, but everyone knows it is to help the congregation huddle together and not miss the many men – fathers, brothers and sons who should be there too.

The Selby family take their places near the front, Edward on the end of the row, by the aisle, so that he can do his duties as church warden. The brass, octagonal collection plate is passed along the pews and the head of every family puts something in the tray. Edward takes the plate to the altar. He hands it to the pastor and kneels down, head bowed. The pastor raises the polished dish with both hands, closes his eyes and prays. 'Father, we thank you…' he begins.

Just then, Edward hears a gasp behind him. It sounds like his wife. He half turns his head, but when no more sounds come, he returns to the prayer. His wife has her hand to her brow, shielding her face as he walks back to the pew. 'What's the matter?' he asks in a whisper. She looks up at him, her eyes streaming with silent tears. 'He's coming home, Edward. I know he is!' she whispers back. 'I felt it in the prayers. He's coming home!'

Edward feels his stomach wrench with hope, but pushes this surging feeling forcefully back. Back to the place where he keeps all the feelings he dares not set free. 'Humph,' he grunts dismissively. Why would *she* feel anything? She is just Reg's stepmother, even if she has known him since he was a little boy. His mother, Alice, Edward's first wife passed away all too soon. Surely *he* as his father would know, if anyone – and he does not feel a thing. Then again, perhaps she is right, perhaps he is coming back. But no. He cannot, should not consider it. And if he does, then in all likelihood it will be in a box, or with part of him blown away. That is how most of the boys return, partly missing in body, or in mind. He stiffens his jaw as he learnt to do a war ago, and inwardly closes that door to lock hope firmly inside. He breathes deeply. Yes, that feels better – to feel nothing, hope for nothing.

But hope seeps through the smallest cracks and he cannot help turning back to look at the cross on the altar as they all file along the aisle out of the church at the end of the service. He turns his eyes to the suffering image of Him who died to save, and mutters softly, 'May it be Your Will to return him safely to us.'

Stepmother she may be, but she dusts the furniture and washes the window and the curtains in Reg's room. Edward looks on as she airs the bed linen, but says nothing to her. 'Let her hope,' he thinks. 'Let her distract herself with preparations. I shall get ready to be there for her when disappointment comes.'

On the morning of Christmas Eve, the telegram boy is up early, ready to do his last round before Christmas Day. The old postman, George, comes into the post office, stamping big chunks of snow from his boots before stepping inside to collect the next big bag of Christmas mail. This winter, it is definitely a white Christmas, he thinks – pretty, but with supplies of fuel so limited, even the children might have preferred a milder year.

'Are you ready for the round?' he asks the boy.

'Yes, sir, just sorting the telegrams now.'

The telegram boy slings his bag over his shoulder and gets on his bike. 'Mind how you go on that! There's too much snow and it's very slippery!' calls the postman.

The boy grins and tugs at his cap. 'Merry Christmas!' he says and slides off down the road, as the postman watches from the door. He has barely turned back to the letters and parcels, when there is a crash and a cry.

Hurrying outside, he sees the telegram boy lying in the snow with his bike on its side and the telegrams scattered across the road. 'What did I say?' puffs George, tutting angrily. He strides over carefully and helps the boy up. Then he stoops to gather the telegrams before their fine paper gets wet on the snow.

'Sorry, sir!' wails the boy.

'As long as you're alright, you silly lad! Go on, get off home with you. But make sure you help your mother instead! It'll be busy in your house!'

'What about the telegrams?'

The old man glances down at the small pile. 'I'll deliver these with the letters. Almost everyone will have post today, so I'll sort these to match the rest.'

'Thank you, Sir,' says the boy and quietly wheels his bike away.

George trudges back into the post office and starts slipping the telegrams in with the other items for the right streets. He spots the name 'Selby' and whips it out from the pile. His heart beats faster and he feels his stomach lurch. He stares at the thin folded paper, his eyes locked on the name. 'A telegram. Today of all days,' he says to himself, a grim look settling over his face. He knows what this almost always means. Glancing at the date, he sees that it should have arrived before today. He tuts and frowns again, picking up his postbag with the rest of the post and sets off up the freezing white lane with heavy tread.

Despite the snow, the late morning train to Ware is pulling into the station on time, steam hissing and the brakes straining to hold back the heavy engine. Reg already has the carriage door partly open and, as the train rocks back to come to a final stop, he sees the snow piled by the walls and jumps lithely onto the well-swept, but still icy platform. He lands safely and strides for the barrier.

'Merry Christmas!' he says to the guard by the gate, a veteran from the Home Guard, who is looking frail in the chill of this wintry morning. He looks up at the young man with blurry eyes, watery in the cold air. He blinks to clear them. He sees the uniform and smart cap and raises an arm to wave. Reg salutes with precision and a big smile, before turning to head out and down the road at pace. 'Ahohah!' The old man tries to clear his throat to speak, but everything works so slowly for him these days. 'Welcome home, son!' he calls croakily, waving stiffly after the disappearing figure of the captain, then blinks his eyes blurred all over again – now with joy – whispers, 'Well! It's young Reg! Come home at last! Heaven be praised! Edward will be so relieved!'

The Selby family are gathering for lunch around their old wooden kitchen table. Edward Selby has already been working for hours and made the last deliveries of carrots and potatoes to the kitchen of the big house for the main Christmas meals to come. He has returned in his gardening clothes to change for the preparations at home. Kathleen is laying the table in her white apron and Victor is polishing his shoes, ready for church. He quickly puts the brushes away when he sees his dad and hurries to wash his hands before he can be declared late at the table – again.

His mother has a large teapot in her hands. She is pouring hot tea into four cups, carefully holding the teapot lid in place, when she hears the noise of someone lifting the gate latch and then their squeaky muffled tread on the newly fallen snow. These familiar sounds interrupt the ticking of the grandmother clock on the wall. 'It'll be the postman' she thinks. 'Late today with all the post to deliver! I hope we'll hear from more family and friends. We could do with some good news!' But instead of the cards and letters being posted through the letterbox, there's a knock on the door. Edward gets up to answer it.

'George! Merry Christmas!' He greets the old postman warmly and puts out his strong hand to shake that of his friend. But George does not smile in response. He takes off his glove and shakes the offered hand, then slips his fingers into his postbag to draw out letters and hand them over. Edward is about to thank him, when George adds, 'There's also this,' and holds out the telegram. It shakes a little in his fingers as he lays it on to Edward's open palm and looks up at him with sadness in his eyes. 'I'm sorry, Edward. It only arrived this morning.' Edward's smile falls away. He frowns and looks at the thin, folded paper.

Deep lines appear around his mouth as he takes the telegram. George stretches out a hand and squeezes Edward's arm. He nods silently to Mrs Selby, turns and walks slowly back out of the gate, stepping into his own snowy footprints. He walks back past the fence and the hedge, his tread feeling weary in the falling snow, and heavy too with the inevitable sorrow that he fears the few typed words will bring. The pattern is almost always the same. The first telegram says 'Missing in Action,' the second confirms that the soldier, loved one, hero is not coming back. There had been hope while he was in the camp, but since Allied Armistice Day in September the previous year, news has been even harder to come by.

Still looking down as he trudges up the road through the rapidly thickening snow, George does not see the young man marching towards him with long energetic strides and a fresh strong energy that belies the worsening weather and slippery snow underfoot. The postman nearly bumps straight into the young man. The soldier holds out a firm hand to steady the old man, then, as the familiar face looks up and is about to cry out, quickly puts a finger across his lips. 'Reg,' whispers George, as involuntary tears fill his eyes, 'Thank God!' Reg pats his arm, silently mouths 'Merry Christmas, George!' grins and winks as he strides past him towards the Round House Lodge, home.

Edward is still standing in the doorway, numb to the cold winter air, when he feels a gentle touch on his arm as he turns to go back inside. His wife is beside him, looking at the sealed telegram fluttering slightly in Edward's trembling hand. Kathleen walks slowly to join them and the three figures stand staring at each other, unable to move.

The young soldier is by the garden gate. He raises his hand to open the latch, and then looks at the post where he used to place his palm to vault it, now covered in a good three inches of snow. He hesitates and frowns a little, as if the memories of all he has been through since he last stood in this place rush across his mind. Then, with a deep breath and the start of a smile, he steps back to take up a well-practised stance and places his hand firmly, instinctively on the old spot and springs over the gate, landing softly on the snow.

He sees his father's back, his stepmother and sister, heads bowed, by the open door. Puzzled at first, he looks back up the road towards George's disappearing figure and realises that his telegram must only just have arrived, George must have brought it. Why don't they look pleased? Haven't they read it? Ah, no – then perhaps they think…

He hears his sister Kath's familiar voice, now sad and timid asking, 'Father, what does it say?'

As if from far away, Reg's strong young voice reaches into the fearful huddle. 'It says,' he explains, 'that I'll be home for Christmas!'

At that moment, up at the top of the road, through the silence of the snow-muffled morning, the postman George hears squeals of joy, cries of delight and relief coming from the garden of the Round House Lodge. He turns back and smiles. He can imagine the hugs, the tears and the trembling hands grabbing at the young man's sleeves, Reg's stepmother holding his face in her hands to check he is really there, Kath pressing in for her turn to hug and hold her big brother, as if never to let him go, and young Victor leaping around in the snowy front garden calling at the top of his voice, 'I said he'd find his way home! I said it! Ha, ha!'

With tears pricking his eyes too, George lets out a cry. He is hit by a wave of relief and pleasure for his old friend, for all the family, for the whole community that knows them in Ware! So many times he has had to deliver a telegram with the news no one wants to receive. Here, now, at last is the greatest joy. 'Merry Christmas, Edward! Merry Christmas to you all!' he says in a quiet, trembling voice, then he too takes a deep breath and laughs out loud as he trudges back through the village in the snow.

14

Coda

Turning back to the warmth of the room in her cosy flat, Beth lets these images fade quickly away. She tidies the last papers back into the folders to put into the old leather suitcase. She slides the fine paper of her grandfather's letter gently back in the envelope, but it will not lie straight. Teasing the sides open, she sees another page, just as fine, partly stuck to the side seal, so she had not found it before. Beth draws it out carefully and reads:

P.S. My story tells you of others on whose graves I should have laid flowers. History shows that it is never too late, and I believe that remembering them is all that they would have asked. Now is the time to seek reconciliation. We need to remember the courage it takes to fight and the loss to all that war brings. Remember, but do not do this to arouse ill feeling – remember in order to cherish what we have that is shared and is good. The spirit of those days must live on in all our descendants so that belief in freedom will never die.

You have come to know my past but this past travels with you into your future. Knowing that this story lives on will help me truly to rest in peace.

Your great-grandfather and your grandfather lived their part in history with hope, courage and shared humanity and these qualities are your inheritance. Now I hope you will feel that my strength and love are always with you.

Your Dadu, Captain Reginald Edward Selby

Returning from the kitchen, her companion on this journey, the smart, funny and sometimes hapless Robert quietly places a cup of coffee on her desk by the old suitcase, and gently places his hand on her shoulder.

Beth turns and for perhaps the first time in the whole journey of discovery, let's out uncontrollable, deep sobs, 'Oh Robert!'

He instinctively puts his arms around her. 'It's alright! In fact, it's wonderful! You have earned all the gratitude in his letter – as he knew you would! You have followed his journey, his story. You found the Chiesa family and you laid flowers, as he wished. So, do you think he is resting in peace now?'

She turns, laying down the letter, looks up at him, smiling and wiping away her tears. She clasps his hand tightly. 'I believe he is, Robert. I believe he is.'

The End

Appendix I

Historical contextual notes

Compensation for Supporters of the Allies

On 11 July 1944, the Allied Screening Commission was set up to compensate those who had helped prisoners of war to escape. Its brief was to recompense citizens: '…giving recognition to and compensating persons in Italy who had assisted Allied personnel behind enemy lines following the Allied Armistice with Italy.'

Over 100,000 claims were processed and 75,000 payments granted, amounting to around £1 million. One claim was permitted per household and evidence was based on reports by POWs or chits and 'I owe yous' left on scraps of paper with the householders.

Reg likewise passed on the names of the households that had helped him, in the expectation that they would be reimbursed at some point and in some way. We have not found specific evidence that this came to pass, but hope that it did.

The Bedfordshire and Hertfordshire Regiment

The Bedfordshire and Hertfordshire Regiment was an infantry regiment of the British Army that traced its origins back to 1688. After long years of service in many campaigns it was merged with The Essex Regiment in 1958 to form the 3rd East Anglian Regiment.

The badge of the Hertfordshire Regiment is the depiction of a hart crossing a ford and was added to the regiment's badge in 1881 after the Hertfordshire Militia was merged into it. The name 'Hertford' derives from the Anglo-Saxon *heort fora*. *Heort* survives in modern English as 'hart', meaning stag, and *ford* as 'ford', a shallow place where animals and humans can walk through a waterway such as a stream or river.

The Hymn, *Eternal Father, Strong to Save*

The words to this hymn were written by William Whiting in 1860, inspired by Psalms 104 and 107 which refer to the dangers of the sea. It became the anthem for sailors and other seafarers.

Eternal Father, strong to save,
Whose arm hath bound the restless wave,
Who bid'st the mighty ocean deep
Its own appointed limits keep;
O hear us when we cry to Thee,
For those in peril on the sea.

O Christ, whose voice the waters heard
And hushed their raging at Thy word,
Who walkedst on the foaming deep,
And calm amidst its rage didst sleep;
O hear us when we cry to Thee,
For those in peril on the sea.

Most Holy Spirit, Who didst brood
Upon the chaos dark and rude,
And bid its angry tumult cease,
And give, for wild confusion, peace;
O hear us when we cry to Thee,
For those in peril on the sea!

O Trinity of love and power,
Our brethren shield in danger's hour;
From rock and tempest, fire and foe,
Protect them wheresoe'er they go;
Thus evermore shall rise to Thee
Glad hymns of praise from land and sea.

Italian Songs

Three songs in particular are known to have been sung, loved and used in their communications by the partisans and the Italian villagers at that time. They were no doubt part of Reg's musical life while in Italy:

Torna a Soriento
Bella Ciao
Fiorellin del Prato

Appendix II

About Captain R. E. Selby

Early Years

Reginald Edward Selby was born on 5 December 1920 at Fanhams Hall Gardens in Ware, Hertfordshire, where his father, Edward, was recorded as working as a Gardener and Manservant (source: birth certificate). It was the home of Lord Croft, Parliamentary Under-Secretary of State for War from 1940 to 1945. Reg, as he was known, and his sister Kathleen lost their mother, Alice Rose Minnie, to illness when they were very young. Edward remarried, and added a step-brother for Reg, called Jack, to his family. Later a younger stepbrother, Victor, was born. Reg did well at grammar school and received a letter exempting him from a matriculation examination to the University of London, but access to further education was overtaken by the advent of World War II. Reg spent most of his twenties at war, joining officially at age 19, in June 1940.

The story told in this book traces his experiences from joining up to returning home from Italy.

Reginald Edward Selby was captured after his company was decimated by the Nazis in North Africa and he was taken, as a prisoner of war, to Italy. When Italy changed sides in 1943, he escaped and was hidden and hosted by local peasant families with the help of the Italian partisans, until it became too dangerous to stay after the death of an Allied évadé during a raid. He was provided with false identity documents and a train ticket. He was told to follow a woman in a red beret, and find the priest and the partisan who would guide him to the border with Switzerland, if only he could make it past the hordes of German soldiers along the way. He was one of the lucky few who escaped successfully. At the end of the war, the political situation in Italy remained unstable, with ongoing risks to those Italians who had helped the Allies, making it potentially dangerous for them to be contacted directly for some years. Time passed, but his gratitude never faded.

His written account is a factual report. Its military-style contents, with its numbered paragraphs were, for the fictionalised narrative content of this book, elaborated on and supplemented by conversations between characters, which though invented are closely based on Reg's own account and notes. The hidden tale of love was shared with us verbally in conversations excluded from his manuscript and this thread runs alongside the account of honour, courage and danger, which this retelling also aims to convey. It is often the tiny details that bring tales to life and one comment I recall is that he found he was never able to eat grapes, even ripe ones, in the years following the war, so strong was the impact of the taste of unripe grapes he had had to eat when on the run from the arriving German forces after the Armistice.

Other soldiers named in this book are either specifically mentioned in Reg's notes or are recorded in other reports as having been in the same places as Reg at the same time, so they are very likely to have met him and had the kind of conversations described here. However, while some of these conversations are based on quotations, others have been devised, as in other parts of the narrative, to bring the facts to life.

Following his escape, Reg was taken to be de-briefed and then assigned a place of residence, which for much of the time was at the Gasthaus Löwen in Ganterschwil, Switzerland, but as an évadé, he was allowed to travel freely and mix with the Swiss population. This enabled him to explore Switzerland in a way that other Allied military personnel were not permitted to do. If RAF pilots had made a forced landing, for example, they were classed as internees and not allowed to leave the Internment Camps. His contemporary notes were, he said, taken away, but we have been unable to trace the official record of them in military archives. He mentioned that he found a notebook that provided many of the facts in his 1986–1987 account, so it seems he made new notes shortly after the war, which he then kept. He was required to stay in Switzerland for some months and given the task of supervising workers from a range of nationalities. On one occasion he enjoyed racing the Swiss troops in a run across the mountains, though he regretfully admitted that he had been unable to beat them! He was however given a Swiss Alpina watch for coming second, which he treasured all his life, not just for its rarity in England at the time, but for its significance to him, which was invaluable. He wore it daily and it was still working in the 1980s, having never been cleaned or repaired.

Service After Italy

After finally returning to the UK on leave, as outlined in this account, Reg's war was not over. He was trained in bomb disposal and redeployed to Patras in Greece, and then served in the 2nd Battalion of the Bedfordshire and Hertfordshire Regiment, British Forces in Greece at Edhessa and the Royal Norfolk Regiment, until the war was finally over. His notes recall that an amusing aspect of his role involved interpretation between the Greeks and the Italians. His schoolboy knowledge of the Greek alphabet (he achieved particular credit in five of his high school examination subjects in 1936, including Greek) helped him to demystify communications written in Greek script, but using the Italian language!

The Italian songs he had learnt, his good looks and quick mind attracted women wherever he went and there are letters from female admirers in a number of countries and in a number of languages amongst the correspondence that he kept.

His skill as a speaker was noted early. As a young officer before deployment, he was asked to represent a fellow soldier in a court-martial and was successful in getting an acquittal, despite the fact that the innocence of the accused was somewhat in doubt. This resulted in further requests for him to represent those similarly accused.

Meanwhile back in England, Reginald's regiment was reformed following its terrible decimation at Monte Cassino. The battles to win that strategic stronghold over four months in 1944 were legendary and it was only won at a great cost on both sides. However, despite being reinforced, the regiment was already in the process of being redistributed and amalgamated into others. The troops found out that they were to be reassigned to other regiments and ultimately, that was the East Anglian. Reg left a selection of wartime maps of Norfolk and East Anglia in his brown leather suitcase.

While still in service, he came to know Lieutenant Terry D. Muirhead. They discussed what they might do after the war and both decided to apply for the SAS. Terry was successful, but Reg was not. One of the activities of his friend is recorded online in a reference to a particular operation known as Archway:

Lt Terry d Muirhead SAS MC Operation Archway
https://en.wikipedia.org/wiki/Operation_Archway

https://sites.google.com/site/operationarchway/home/nominal-roll-of-personnel-2nd-sas-squadron-appendix-a-continued

After the War

P/197146.   18th December 1946.

Sir,

    Now that the time has come for your release from
active military duty, I am commanded by the Army Council
to express to you their thanks for the valuable services
which you have rendered in the service of your country
at a time of grave national emergency.

    At the end of the emergency you will relinquish
your commission, and at that time a notification will
appear in the London Gazette (Supplement), granting you
also the honorary rank of Captain. Meanwhile, you have
permission to use that rank with effect from the date of
your release.

                    I am, Sir,

                        Your obedient Servant,

Captain R.E.Selby,
The Bedfordshire and Hertfordshire Regiment.

Confirmation of honorary title of Captain. (Family archive)

Reg was finally officially discharged from military service on 26 February 1947. However, he was granted leave in early December 1946 and immediately travelled to marry his first wife in Ireland on 9 December of that year. The marriage did not last, and the couple later parted on amicable terms, and she, Mary, is believed to have emigrated to America.

Subject: Class "A" Release.

To: The Adjutant, 4 Bn. Royal Norfolk Regiment.

From: 197146 T/Capt. R.E. Selby. A.& S. Gp. 31 DV6.

       I beg to submit this my application to return to England at least a week before my date for Release.

       My Age and Service Group Number is 31 DV6, and I am therefore due to be released on 16 Dec., 46. I deferred six months to proceed to Greece with 4 Bn. Royal Norfolk Regt., and this Unit is now disbanding.

       I am getting married in Dublin on 20 Dec., 46, and have, in addition to the usual arrangements entailed, the extra difficulty of securing the necessary documents for my passage to Eire.

       Moreover, I have to be back in England at the beginning of January, 1947, in order to attend a Business Administrative Course commencing at that time.

Patras.
14 Sept., 46.

Request for early release due to wedding. (Family archive)

Early in 1947, Reg attended a government-backed General Business Training Course, arranged by the Ministry of Labour. He received an excellent reference from his commanding officer, the regiment's Lieutenant Colonel. The typed document is pinned to the handwritten reference, drafted on extremely thin sheets of paper and also signed by the officer.

On release, he was granted permission to use the title of captain in civilian life, but chose not to do so. He had been recommended for promotion to major in the autumn of 1946, since this was the normal rank for his final role as an H.Q. Company commander, but it seems that this did not proceed to completion, perhaps because he was in any case about to be discharged. The title he took into civilian life was that of captain.

TO WHOM IT MAY CONCERN.

Capt.R.E.Selby. The Bedfordshire & Hertfordshire Regiment.

          The above mentioned Officer served under me as
Adjutant. He is conscientious, and extremely hard working.Above
the average intelligence, he possess initiative to a marked
degree. Most reliable and loyal to his superiors. He has also a
very pleasant disposition and a sense of humour. I have no
doubt but that he will do well in any walk of life he finds
himself in. On his departure I feel I am losing not only a good
Adjutant, but a cheerful and loyal comrade.

                                              Lt Col.
          Commanding 2nd Bn Bedfordshire &Hertfordshire Regt.
                                  British Forces in Greece.
                                  24 Nov., 46.

Reference from his commanding officer. (Family archive)

The sponsored training course, on which Reg won a place, was in Ireland. It was a near two-year apprenticeship working in the new industry of data management, initially for Powers-Samas Accounting Machines Limited. He performed well and received an offer of a permanent post as Technical Advisor, dated 23 December 1947, for a salary of £500 per annum, more than doubling his previous pay of £16 8s 4d per month as a married officer and trainee.

In his letters, he talks of his excitement at seeing processes automated for the first time.

While working there, he met and fell in love with a striking young woman from England who was also employed in this new industry, Zenia Luxton. She was in charge of the pool of female administrators who supported the data managers. Reg and Zenia were married after his divorce came through, in a civil ceremony in 1954 in Blackpool and together they had three sons, Paul, Mark and Neil. Zenia and Reg remained devoted to each other until his death fifty years later. Reg's career advanced within the computing industry and he reached the position of Marketing Director at ICL (International Computers Limited). He retired at age 60, following a heart attack. However, he wanted to continue to be commercially active. He revised and updated his knowledge of accountancy – acquired in the Italian POW camp – and used it to offer support services and advice to local businesses part-time in his adopted home city of Manchester. He continued this work into his early seventies, after which his memory began to fail. His wife Zenia cared for him until the very last stages of his decline. Even in the final months of his dementia, he still remembered all the words to the Italian songs he had learnt as an escapee and sang them to Zenia. Reg died in 2005 and the funeral service was held as described in this story.

RELEASE - OFFICERS

Personal Number...19.7.146... Present Rank TEMP./CAPT.
(Acting or Temp)

Surname...SELBY...Christian Names REGINALD EDWARD.
(in full)

Parent Regt......BEDFS. & HERTS.

Age/Service Group...31 DV6...Date of Birth...5 DEC., 1920...

Permanent Address (if not known, Temporary Address)
......ROUND House LODGE, HIGH OAK ROAD......
.........WARE., HERTFORDSHIRE..........
(COUNTY)........

Higher Rank held........... Date of Relinquishment...............

Have deductions for National Health Insurance been made from Pay (State YES or NO) ...YES......

Were you commissioned from the ranks ...YES.........
Date..11. JULY.'41.   Army No...595.5945......
Previously had Unemployment Book....NO.......(YES or NO)

Date of Commission on joining from Reserve or Unemployment List ....

If you have served in Ranks give Army No or Militia No...5955945.
Date of Commencement of Effective Service (incl OR Service)14 JUNE, 40

Single or Married, etc...SINGLE... Med Cat......A1.

Type of Commission.EMERGENCY.Rank on Release....CAPT.........

Condition on Release...UNEMPLOYMENT.
(See Appx to GRO 1200/45)

Nationality......ENGLISH..........

Nearest Post Office to Home Address..WARE., HERTS.........

Agent or Paymaster..GLYN. MILLS & Co., HOLT's BRANCH.....

NB - STRICT ACCURACY IS ESSENTIAL WHEN COMPLETING
     THIS FORM

Officers' Release Certificate, Captain R. E. Selby. (Family archive)

Appendix III

Further Images and Photos
Relevant to The Story

The camp at Fontanellato, photographed in 1987. It was originally built to be an orphanage, but was made into a camp for Allied POWs in 1943 (The Author CCBY)

QUESTA LAPIDE RICORDA
NEL QUARANTESIMO ANNIVERSARIO
I PRIGIONIERI DI GUERRA
INGLESI E ALLEATI
QUI INTERNATI NEL CAMPO
DI CONCENTRAMENTO P.G. 49
LA POPOLAZIONE DI
FONTANELLATO
CHE DOPO L' ARMISTIZIO
DEL 8 SETTEMBRE 1943
LI AIUTO' E LI NASCOSE
A RISCHIO DI
GRAVI RAPPRESAGLIE

FONTANELLATO 11 SETTEMBRE 1983

Commemorative plaque on the gates, photographed in 1987. (The Author CCBY)
Text on the Plaque (Translation by the Author)
On the 40th anniversary of the Armistice of 8th September 1943, this plaque
commemorates the English and Allied Prisoners of War who were held at
Concentration Camp P.G. 49, and the inhabitants of Fontanellato who helped them
and hid them despite the risk of grave repercussions.
11 November 1983

The graves of Marina and Domenico Chiesa, 1987. (The Author CCBY)

The landscape of Pellegrino Parmense in 1987. (The Author CCBY)

Officers and NCOs of the 1st Battalion, Beds and Herts Regiment in camp at the airship base at Cardington, Bedfordshire around 1925. It was reported that the R-100 was at its masthead nearby. Edward Selby is in row three, far left. (Family Archive Photograph, Family records)

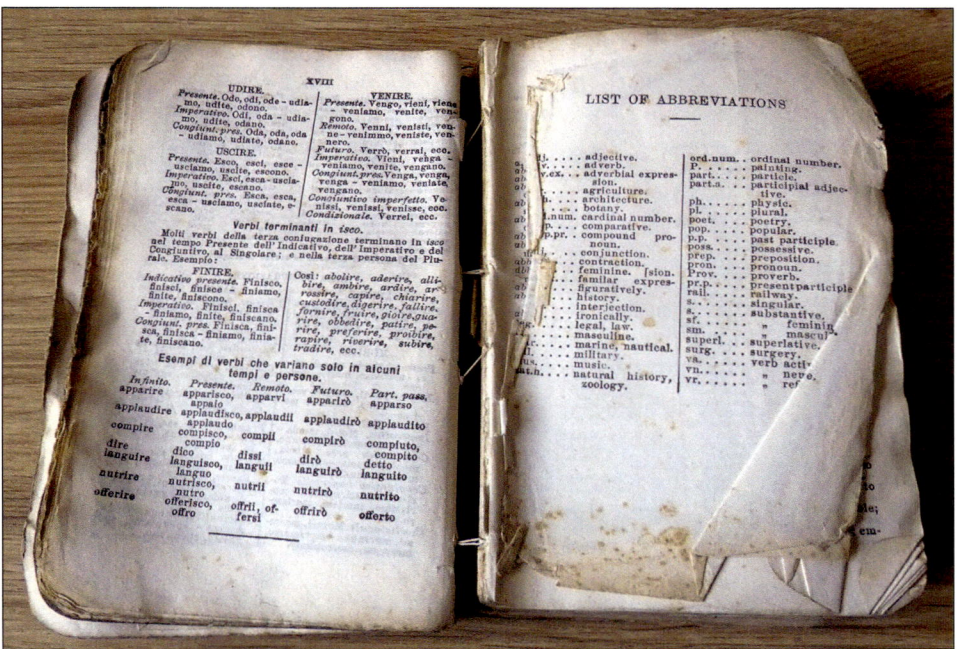

Inside pages of the crinkled Italian dictionary. (The Author CCBY)

R. E. Selby Driving Licence from 1953. While permissions for all vehicles were obtained during service, the paperwork followed only after the war. His 1953–1954 permit does however confirm that he remained licensed to ride a motorbike as well as cars. (The Author CCBY)

The Round House Lodge where Reg lived as a boy with his father Edward. Photo taken by Reg in 1988. (Family Archive Photograph, Family records)

Bibliography and Main References

Churchill, Winston S., *The Second World War Volume III, The Grand Alliance, 1950,* (London: The Reprint Society, Seventh impression, November 1954)

Churchill, Winston S, *The Second World War Volume III, the Grand Alliance* (Boston, MA: Houghton Mifflin, USA, 1951), p.161

Churchill, Winston S., 1951, *The Second World War, Volume V, Closing the Ring* (Boston, MA: Houghton Mifflin, USA, 1951), pp.166–167

Hallpike-Selby, Claire Diana and Neil Selby, *Retracing the Escape Route – travel notes* 1987 (Personal record of research trip, unpublished)

Holland, James, *Italy's Sorrow* (London: Harper Press, 2009)

Lao Tzu, Tao Te Ching (Ralph Alan Duke, trans.) *Verse 50, The Forces of Life and Death* (London: Watkins Publishing, 2008)

McNab, Chris, *The World War I Story* (London: The History Press, 2011)

Miller, John, *Friends and Romans* (London: Grafton Books, 1989)

Newby, Eric, *Love and War in the Apennines* (London: Harper Collins, 1971)

Remarque, Erich Maria, *Im Westen Nichts Neues* (Cologne: Kiepenheuer & Witsch GmbH & Co KG, 1959)

Hood, Stuart, *Pebbles from my Skull* (London: Hutchinson & Co, 1963)

Ross, Michael, *The British Partisan,* (Barnsley: Pen and Sword Books, 1997)

Selby, Captain Reginald E. (written by Zenia Selby, née Luxton, from dictation by Reginald), *Account of my Wartime Service,* 1987 (Personal memoir, unpublished)

Tudor, Malcolm, *Escape from Italy 1943–45,* (Newtown: Emilia Publishing, 2003)

Tudor, Malcolm, *Prisoners and Partisans,* (Newtown: Emilia Publishing, 2006)

Tudor, Malcolm, *At War in Italy 1943–45* (Newtown: Emilia Publishing, 2007)

Tudor, Malcolm, *Beyond the Wire* (Newtown: Emilia Publishing, 2009)

Tudor, Malcolm, *British Prisoners of War in Italy – Paths to Freedom,* (Newtown: Emilia Publishing, 2012)

Tudor, Malcolm, *Among the Italian Partisans* (Stroud: Fonthill Media Limited, 2016)

Website: https://ww2escapelines.co.uk, Accessed 21 December 2024

Editorial Comments

I would like to draw upon the greater experience and expertise of Robert Harris to express my excuses and reasons for the choices made in the writing of this story.

> All the errors that remain, factual and stylistic, along with the various sleights of hand in narrative and characterisation invariably required to turn fact into fiction, remain my sole responsibility.
> Robert Harris, *An Officer and a Spy* (Stratford upon Avon: Arrow, 2013)

For the purposes of keeping the storyline clear for the modern reader, the order of some parts has been slightly adjusted from the original notes. An example is that the bus journey within the escape route occurred in Reg's report after the church service, but it was better for the momentum of the journey to present the service as the last destination point before the border. Since escape routes were varied to avoid detection and the exact path beyond Milan is unclear, the change in the order of points on the journey was made, along with this note by way of explanation.

The scenes in the Round House Lodge are reimagined based on the author's having spent family time with Kathleen, Victor and Reg himself, and hearing tales from their youth. The scenes in the home of the Chiesa family are based on the anecdotes that Reg shared verbally after the written account of his escape had been dictated in 1986–1987 to his wife. His affection for Maria and the details of their potential betrothal were omitted from those written notes out of respect for his wife of many decades, Zenia, née Luxton. She took down the notes in dictation and they are recorded in her very artistic handwriting.

However, he shared his strong emotions about the Chiesa family in conversations with the explorers from the next generation, so that they could carry his wishes to Italy on an investigative journey that followed his escape route in 1987. Reg asked the researchers to check that Domenico and Marina had lived out their lives to a good age after the end of hostilities and that Maria was alive and well. Tracing that path in Emilia-Romagna led his son Neil and daughter-in-law Claire Diana to encounters with locals who had been part of the resistance, the *partigiani*. The tales they told are the basis of the conversations reproduced here in the town centre piazza and village café. The incident of the reluctance of villagers to have anything to do with Neil and Claire Diana until they realised they were English and not German is completely true. The trip enabled us to confirm that the Chiesa parents had lived into their seventies and that their daughter Maria still worked in the area. After his family's research trip in Italy, Reg attempted to contact the two sons in the Chiesa family, Guido and Gianni, but to no avail.

Later still, Reg's granddaughters, the elder named Zenia after his wife, and her younger sister Helena, were taken as teenagers to visit the area in Emilia-Romagna, the towns and villages, the graveyards and vineyards, to feel the sun, smell the air and see the landscape – abundant and peaceful.

The suitcase of documents had been lost and forgotten for many years. Its existence was unknown to the family until found in the loft of the family home and retrieved shortly before Reg's passing, when he was sadly no longer well enough to answer the many questions that came to mind.

This retelling draws together many threads. At its core lies the factual account dictated by Reg himself. The colour and detail have been drawn from the two research trips made by the next generation, supplemented with research at the military archives in the Imperial War Museum, the pop-up Regimental Museum in 2014/2015, the accounts of many other survivors (see bibliography), the recollections of other family members, such as stepbrother Victor's wife and the many documents from the suitcase, some of which are reproduced here.

In order to match the narrative to habits of the time, Reg's name appears largely as follows: Reg as a boy to his family and friends in the village of Ware; Reg to his fellow soldiers and POWS; Reggie to his wife and their grown up children; and Reginald in official documents. It is believed that he was affectionately referred to as Reggio by the Italians, but there is no documentary evidence to that effect.

Where the names of the other parties are known, these are used, such as for Paolo the barber's assistant. Where the names are not known, for the purposes of the story, possible names have been introduced. The specific name of the guide who took Reg to the border with Switzerland is not known. Reg believed he heard that the man he met had been tortured to death after the enemy discovered that he had helped Allied men to escape recapture. However, it is reported that a person called Umbertino Granata undertook a similar high risk role as a guide in the area of Lake Maggiore, so his name is used here in tribute to all those brave Italians without whose help many more lives would have been lost.

Every effort has been made to make the story appear natural and chronological.